Richard Talbert, Kai B

Space in the Roman World

Antike Kultur und Geschichte

herausgegeben von

Prof. Dr. Kai Brodersen

(Universität Mannheim)

Band 5

LIT

Richard Talbert, Kai Brodersen (Eds.)

Space in the Roman World

Its Perception and Presentation

LIT

Bibliographic information published by Die Deutsche Bibliothek
Die Deutsche Bibliothek lists this publication in the Deutsche
Nationalbibliografie; detailed bibliographic data are available in the
Internet at http://dnb.ddb.de.

ISBN 3-8258-7419-2

© LIT VERLAG Münster   2004
Grevener Str./Fresnostr. 2   48159 Münster
Tel. 0251-23 50 91   Fax 0251-23 19 72
e-Mail: lit@lit-verlag.de   http://www.lit-verlag.de

Distributed in North America by:

Transaction Publishers
New Brunswick (U.S.A.) and London (U.K.)

Transaction Publishers
Rutgers University
35 Berrue Circle
Piscataway, NJ 08854

Tel.: (732) 445 - 2280
Fax: (732) 445 - 3138
for orders (U. S. only):
toll free (888) 999 - 6778

Table of Contents

Antike Kultur und Geschichte
(Ancient Culture and History)

The series presents new studies on ancient culture and history, in monographs and collections of general historical interest. All volumes are published by LIT and available through bookshops and directly from www.lit-verlag.de. Volumes previously published in this series include:

Gebet und Fluch, Zeichen und Traum: Aspekte religiöser Kommunikation in der Antike. Ed. by Kai Brodersen. (AKG, vol. 1, 2001; 120 pp., ISBN 3-8258-5352-7, € 20.90)

Five original studies on prayers and curses, portents and dreams by Kai Brodersen, Veit Rosenberger, Jörg Rüpke, Tanja Scheer, and Gregor Weber.

Prognosis: Studien zur Funktion von Zukunftsvorhersagen in Literatur und Geschichte seit der Antike. Ed. by Kai Brodersen. (AKG, vol. 2, 2001; 141 pp., ISBN 3-8258-5341-1, € 20.90)

Seven original studies on the function of prognosis in literature and history in the ancient world, and beyond, by Julia Kindt, Sjoerd Levelt, Michael Maaß, Daniel Ogden, Karen Piepenbrink, Veit Rosenberger, and Tanja Scheer

Speculum Regis: Studien zur Fürstenspiegel-Literatur in der griechisch-römischen Antike. By J. Manuel Schulte. (AKG, vol. 3, 2001; 292 pp., ISBN 3-8258-5249-0, € 25.90)

A wide-ranging source-based study of the literary tradition of specula regis from Homer to Marcus Aurelius.

Die Antike außerhalb des Hörsaals. Ed. by Kai Brodersen. (AKG, vol. 4, 2003; 176 pp., ISBN 3-8258-6852-4, € 19.90)

Nine original studies on the Ancient World "outside the lecture-hall" – in the opera and in national monuments, in books for children and young people, in the cinema and in detective novels, and, for the times of the Nazi regime, on flyers distributed by the Weiße Rose and on Victor Ehrenberg's emigration. With contributions by Kai Brodersen, Stefanie Eichler, Nadia Endl, Daniela Evers, Rosmarie Günther, Niklas Holzberg, Stefan Kipf, Ralf Krebs, and Susanna Phillippo.

Preface

How was space perceived and presented in the Roman world? While it is tempting to assume that any modern historical atlas, with its maps of "the world as the Romans saw it", gives a sufficient answer to these questions, recent research has suggested that the issues are more complex than this.

To follow up such questions in more detail, the five original contributions to this volume deal first with the tradition of scientific geography, and especially its two major representatives Eratosthenes, in a study by Klaus Geus (Universität Bamberg/Germany), and Ptolemy, in an essay by Alfred Stückelberger (Universität Bern/Switzerland).

Roman itinerary literature is then explored by Benet Salway (University College London/England) on sea and river travel in this genre, and David Hunt (University of Durham/England) on Holy Land itineraries.

Finally, Richard Talbert (University of North Carolina at Chapel Hill/USA) discusses cartography and taste in the *Tabula Peutingeriana*.

The core of the present volume are lectures given at the 2001 Roman Archaeology Conference in a panel which we had organised on "the perception and presentation of space in the Roman world". We thank the organisers of this conference, and especially Peter van Dommelen (Department of Archaeology, University of Glasgow/Scotland) Benet Salway, David Hunt and Richard Talbert have revised, and expanded, their contributions in the light of the participants' contributions in the lively discussions in Glasgow, and more recent research. Pressures of work have prevented the inclusion of two further papers, Colin Adams (University of Leicester/England) on *Travel and pilgrimage in Roman Egypt: the evidence of 'proskynemata'* and Roger Batty (Keio University/Japan) on *Traditions and reputations in Roman geography*. We are, on the other hand, very pleased to publish in this volume two specially commissioned articles, by Klaus Geus and Alfred Stückelberger on ancient 'scientific' geography, and hope that the English presentation of their thoughts will contribute to an even wider appreciation of their research which has mainly been published in German to date.

For providing the illustrations at the end of this volume we are especially grateful to Tom Elliott (Ancient World Mapping Center, University of North Carolina, Chapel Hill) for 10, 11a, 13-18 (after the series of photographs published by Angerer and Göschl, Vienna 1888), 12 (after *Syria* 6, 1925, pl. 1), and 19 (after M.R. Salzman, *On Roman Time: The Codex-Calendar of 354 and the Rhythms of Urban Life in Late Antiquity*, Berkeley 1990, figs. 13-14), Klaus Geus (Universität Bamberg) for figs. 1-3, Benet Salway (University College London) for figs. 8 (after J. Morton, *The Role of the Physical Environment in Ancient Greek Seafaring*, Mnemosyne Suppl. 213, Leiden 2001, figs. 21 and 23), 9, and 11b (after W.M. Calder and G.E. Bean, *A Classical Map of Asia Minor*, London 1958), and Alfred Stückelberger (Universität Bern) for figs. 4-7.

We are grateful to the Universität Mannheim for supporting this publication, and to the Leverhulme Trust for enabling Kai Brodersen to prepare the publication of this book during a Visiting Fellowship in the School of Greek, Latin, and Ancient History, University of St.Andrews, Scotland, and the School's hospitality. We also wish to thank the publishers, especially Alexander Heck and Frank Weber, for their professional support. Our greatest thanks go to our fellow contributors to the book: Klaus Geus, David Hunt, Benet Salway, and Alfred Stückelberger.

Universität Mannheim / Germany   *Kai Brodersen*
University of North Carolina, Chapel Hill /USA   *Richard Talbert*

The Tradition of Scientific Geography

Measuring the Earth and the *Oikoumene* : zones, meridians, *sphragides* and some other geographical terms used by Eratosthenes of Cyrene

Klaus Geus

Alexandria was the undisputed centre of the scientific world in Hellenistic times. Information from everywhere was brought together here, as it had been at Miletos when Greek colonization was at its height. Ptolemy III Euergetes was even supposed to have issued an order that all books found on ships unloading at Alexandria were to be seized and copied.[1] It is hardly conceivable that these searches produced rare books of literary merit which were not already available in the city's huge library. If the story is true, it must be assumed that Ptolemy was not primarily interested in works of poetry and fiction, but rather in travelogues, diaries and *periploi*. The librarian to whom the king entrusted the inventory and appraisal of the books was Eratosthenes of Cyrene (276-194 BC). His choice was a good one. This multi-talented poet, mathematician, grammarian, astronomer and geographer was especially suitable for such an assignment. In addition to his unusually broad erudition, he had a good eye for the selection of sources, as well as the will to dismiss outdated dogmas.

The scientific works of Eratosthenes are lost. However, later geographers, astronomers, mathematicians and other authors preserve a good number of fragments. Even so, we lack a precise idea of Eratosthenes' concepts, since several sources are inconsistent or use different terms. This is especially true for the astronomical and geographical fragments.

---

[1] Gal. comm. in Hipp. epidem. III (CMG V 10, 2, 1, p. 79 Wenkebach); cf. P.M. Fraser, *Ptolemaic Alexandria*, 2 vols., Oxford 1972, I 325 and II 480-1.

Eratosthenes secured his place in the history of scientific thought with his calculation of the circumference of the earth, based not on conjecture but on mathematics and astronomy.[2] It emerges from different sources, notably from the astronomer Kleomedes, that his method was based on a simple proportion relating the difference between the latitudes of two places on the same meridian (obtained from celestial observations) and their terrestrial distance apart. Eratosthenes determined the circumference of the earth from the following data:

1. the distance between Syene and Alexandria is 5,000 stades;
2. Syene and Alexandria lie on the same meridian;
3. on summer solstice at Syene at noon there is no shadow, because the sun is directly overhead;
4. at the same time at Alexandria the shadow cast by a gnomon in a *skaphe* (a kind of a sundial) reaches an arc equaling 1/50th of a full circle.

This remarkably simple proportion (1/50° : 360° = 5,000 stades : x) led to the conclusion that the circumference of the earth is 50 x 5,000 stades or 250,000 stades (cf. fig. 1).

In the opinion of ancient astronomers and geographers, Eratosthenes' method was solid and his measurement the best possible. The elder Pliny (NH II 247) offered warm praise: *inprobum ausum, verum ita subtili argumentatione conprehensum, ut pudeat non credere.* Even so, we hear of anonymous dissenters.[3] Strabo (c. 64 BC - after 23 AD), our main

---

[2]   K. Geus, *Eratosthenes von Kyrene: Studien zur hellenistischen Kultur- und Wissenschaftsgeschichte*, Munich 2002, 223-38; cf. id., 'Eratosthenes', in: W. Hübner (ed.), *Geographie und verwandte Wissenschaften*, Stuttgart 2000, 75-92, and see G. Dragoni, *Eratostene e l'apogeo della scienza greca*, Bologna 1979; G. Aujac, *Ératosthène de Cyrène, le pionnier de la géographie: Sa mesure de la circonférence terrestre*, Paris 2001.

[3]   Vitr. I 6, 11; Strabo II 4, 1 C 62; cf. II 5, 7 C 113; cf. O.A.W. Dilke, *Greek and Roman Maps*, London 1985, 37. Hipparchos (on whom see D.R. Dicks, *The Geographical Fragments of Hipparchus*, London 1960) accepted Eratosthenes' calculation, but criticized some of his notions which he considered

source for Eratosthenes' geographical achievements,[4] goes so far as to give a totally different explanation of how a geographer measures the earth's circumference:

> By accepting these principles, then, and also by making use of the sundial and the other aids given him by the astronomer – by means of which are found, for the several inhabited localities, both the circles parallel to the equator and the circles that cut the former at right angles, the latter being drawn through the poles (i.e. the meridians) – the geometrician can measure the inhabited portion of the earth by doing fieldwork himself, and the rest of the earth by his calculation of the intervals. In this way he can find the distance from the equator to the pole, which is a fourth part of the earth's largest circle; when he has the distance, he multiplies it by four; and this is the circumference of the earth.   (Strabo II 5, 4 C 111-12).

Here, Strabo did not say a word about Eratosthenes' ingenious method. His own recommendations show that he did not understand mathematical geography nor even the procedure of surveyors. How should an astronomer of Hellenistic times have gathered geodetic readings at the north pole or at the equator?

Consequently, scholars as early as Berger in 1880,[5] assumed that Eratosthenes wrote about his measurement of the earth more than once: he only cites the results in his *Geographika*, but he also described his method elsewhere. This conjecture was indeed proved by Nissen a century ago.[6] There were at least two different books by Eratosthenes

---

mathematically inconsistent or impossible. Cf. fr. 36. 36. 39 Dicks. The elder Pliny tells us that Hipparchos added 26,000 stades to Eratosthenes' 252,000 (NH II 108 = fr. 38 Dicks; note on p. 153). Presumably, he confused two of Eratosthenes' contentions, namely that the equator measures four times 63,000 stades (cf. Strabo II 5, 7 C 113), and that the width of the oikoumene is 38,000 stades. Cf. H. Berger, *Die geographischen Fragmente des Eratosthenes*, Leipzig 1880, 130; D.J. Campbell, *C. Plinii Secundi Naturalis Historiae liber secundus*, Aberdeen 1936, 91.

[4]   On Strabo in general see now D. Dueck, *Strabo of Amaseia*, London 2000.
[5]   Berger op. cit. 119-20.
[6]   H. Nissen, 'Die Erdmessung des Eratosthenes', in: *Rheinisches Museum für*

concerning geography and geodesy, one entitled *About the measurement of the earth*, the other *Geographika*.[7]

The following questions arise from this finding: what is the exact content of each book, which issues are discussed, and what methods are employed? We can reconstruct the composition of the *Geographika* from Strabo with relative ease. Eratosthenes touched upon the following themes: the history of geography (including Homer's eminence); sphericity of the earth; ratio of water and earth; size and position of the oikoumene; diaphragma; parallel circles and meridians; "seals"; description of individual countries; correction of the map of the oikoumene.

A passage in Galen's *Institutio* gives the impression that Eratosthenes at least discussed the following issues in his *About the measurement of the earth*:[8] the length of the earth's circumference, distance of the tropics and polar circles; size and distance of the moon and the sun; total and partial eclipses of the moon and the sun; obliquity of the ecliptic, and

---

Philologie 58, 1903, 231-245, at 232. Heron bears witness to the existence of a second book (dioptr. 35, p. 302, 16 sq. Schoene): Ἐρατοσθένης ἐν <τῷ> ἐπιγραφομένῳ περὶ τῆς ἀναμετρήσεως τῆς γῆς; cf. also Macr. somn. I 20, 9.

[7] In all likelihood Strabo knew both books, but he cites the *Geographika* almost exclusively, and simply expected his readers to know Eratosthenes' major achievement *About the measurement of the earth* (cf. I 1, 20 C 11).

[8] Cf. Geus op. cit. 223-4 (discussing Gal. inst. 12, 2-3). Strabo's statement seems to point in the same direction (I 1, 20 C 11): "It seems to me that, we need, most of all, as I have mentioned, geometry and astronomy for a subject like geography; and the need for them is real indeed; for without such methods as they offer it is not possible to determine accurately our geometrical figures, klimata, dimensions (σχήματα γὰρ καὶ κλίματα καὶ μεγέθη), and also the other cognate items; but just as these sciences prove for us in other treatises all that has to do with the measurement of the earth as a whole (ὥσπερ τὰ περὶ τὴν ἀναμέτρησιν τῆς ὅλης γῆς ἐν ἄλλοις δεικνύουσιν), so I must in this treatise take for granted and accept the propositions proved there (ἐνταῦθα δὲ ὑποθέσθαι δεῖ καὶ πιστεῦσαι τοῖς ἐκεῖ δειχθεῖσιν)." It is true that Strabo does not name Eratosthenes explicitly here, but the relation to *About the measurement of the earth* is nevertheless clear. Strabo had read more of Eratosthenes than the *Geographika*. Cf. I 2, 2 C 15.

(presumably) windrose.[9] Galen (inst. log. 12, 2) even seems to imply that Eratosthenes discussed the earth's zones.

The latter system, described fully by Strabo, can be traced back to the philosopher Parmenides of Elea (c. 500-450 BC), who divided the earth into zones which extended round it in broad bands:[10] there were five zones, two habitable and three uninhabitable. The Greeks lived in the zone "towards the upper pole", which was bounded by the Arctic Circle in the north and the Tropic of the Cancer in the south. Another habitable zone existed towards the South Pole (Strabo II 5, 3 C 111). Since Parmenides lacked any figure for the earth's circumference, he was accordingly unable to determine the size of the zones. Eratosthenes was the first person who could do so, and he presumably had the model illustrated in fig. 2 in mind (in order to simplify the division, Eratosthenes increased his figure *computandi causa* from 250,000 to 252,000 stades).[11]

To make his calculation, Eratosthenes devised "sixtieths" (ἑξήκοντα). Division of the earth's circumference into such sixtieths produced

---

[9] Geus op. cit. 223-38.

[10] Cf. Strabo II 3, 2 C 97, also I 4, 6 C 65 sq.; II 5, 13 C 118.

[11] The figure 250,000 is also mentioned by Philoponos (in meteor. I 3, p. 15 Hayduck [from Arrianos]) and Nikephoros Blemmydes (epit. phys. 339 [PG 142, 1277]). Cf. further Comment. in Arat. rel. p. 125-6 Maass; schol. Dion. Perieg. (GGM II 457); Anon. geogr. expos. comp. fr. A 2 (GGM II 510); slightly different is Hippolyt. haeres. IV 8, 6: 250,543 stades. More often the figure 252,000 is cited. Cf. Vitr. I 6, 9; Strabo II 5, 7 C 113; 5, 34 C 132; Plin. NH II 247-8.; Theo Smyrn. p. 124, 10-12; 127, 19 Hiller; Gal. inst. log. 12, 2; Cens. 13, 2; Mart. Cap. VI 596 (cf. 609); Anon. mens. tot. terr. 1 (GGM I 424); Gerbert. geometr. 93. Cf. Gemin. isag. 16, 6 (and elsewhere); Macr. somn. II 6, 3; Anon. geogr. expos. comp. 1 (GGM II 494). The variant 259,000 goes back to an error in the tradition (Marc. peripl. mar. ext. 4 [GGM I 519]). Capella (VIII 858; but cf. VI 596) ascribed to Archimedes and Eratosthenes the curious figure 406,010. See O. Neugebauer, *A History of Ancient Mathematical Astronomy*, 3 vols., Berlin 1975, II, 651. The figures 250,000 and 252,000 are firmly rooted in the tradition; there can be no doubt that both go back to Eratosthenes.

"intervals" of 4,200 stades each. He then reckoned eight sixtieths or 33,600 stades for the "torrid" zone, seven sixtieths or 29,400 stades for the two "temperate" zones, and four sixtieths or 16,800 stades for the two "frigid" zones. Hence in *About the measurement of the earth* he was already employing the figure 252,000, which matches simple division into sixtieths[12] (division into 360 degrees was only introduced to Greek geography at the earliest by Hipparchos [c. 194-120 BC]).[13]

Eratosthenes modified, or rather superseded, this system in his *Geographika*. Here, instead of the "temperate" zone (ζώνη εὔκρατος), he measured the oikoumene (οἰκουμένη). His method of determining the extremities of the regions is different, too. Strabo tells us how he determined the width of the oikoumene, i.e. the distance between the most northern and most southern points of the known world:

> Next, in determining the width of the oikoumene, Eratosthenes says that, beginning at Meroe and measuring on the meridian that runs through Meroe, it is 10,000 stades to Alexandria; and thence to the Hellespont about 8,100; then to the Borysthenes 5,000; then to the parallel circle that runs through Thule (...) about 11,500. Accordingly, if we add 3,400 more to the south of Meroe, in order to embrace the island of the (fugitive) Egyptians, the Cinnamon-producing country, and Taprobane, we shall have 38,000 stades. (Strabo I 4, 2 C 62-3)

Eratosthenes thus calculated the width of the oikoumene as 38,000 stades, a total that combines known and estimated distances (10,000 + 8,100 + 5,000 + 11,500 + 3,400). In comparable fashion he calculated the length of the oikoumene, determining it to be 77,800 stades (Strabo I 4, 5 C 64); the length thus greatly exceeds the width. So Eratosthenes concluded that the ratio between length (from west to east) and width (from north to south) is "more than 2 : 1".[14]

---

[12] For a different opinion cf. Geus op. cit. 234, n. 117.

[13] Cf. D.R. Dicks, *Early Greek Astronomy to Aristotle*, London 1985, 23. Eratosthenes' contemporaries Aristarchos and Archimedes did not use this division. Cf. Neugebauer op. cit. I 305, n. 27; II, 590. 734-5.

[14] Agathem. I 2 [GGM II 471]; cf. Strabo I 4, 5 C 65. Demokritos proposed a ratio of 1,5 : 1 for the relationship between the oikoumene's length and

Comparing the calculations in both his books, we can easily see that the width of the oikoumene in the *Geographika* (38,000 stades) far exceeds the dimensions of the "temperate" zone (29,400 stades). The abstract system used in *About the measurement of the earth* – one based on mathematical and astronomical principles – was no longer valid by the time that the *Geographika* appeared. We may infer that contemporary voyages (like those of Pytheas or Nearchos), which proved the oikoumene to be inhabited in its furthest north and south, compelled Eratosthenes to give up his old system and to adopt his new one based on travelogues.

The shift in his viewpoint is clear. In *About the measurement of the earth* he tried to measure the whole earth and its zones; in the *Geographika* he looked at the oikoumene and its parts. The methods he applied were different as well. The circumference of the earth was measured astronomically and mathematically, but the oikoumene was measured hodologically, i.e. by means of adding up single distances which Eratosthenes found in sources such as *periploi*, itineraries, geographical works.

It is easy to see that the accuracy of Eratosthenes' description of the oikoumene depends on the quality of his sources. The astronomer Hipparchos criticized this aspect of his method, and insisted that all fixed points on a map needed to be measured astronomically. Legitimate as such a demand was, lack of technical expertise made it impossible to fulfil in antiquity. To that extent, Eratosthenes' scientifically more modest approach was justified.

Having determined the size of the oikoumene, he then ventured to determine its respective parts and to put their features on a map (of the oikoumene alone, not of the whole earth!). As already indicated above, he used meridians and parallel circles as outlines for this rectangular map. While the five zones were astronomically determined by

its width (VS 68 B 15 = Agathem. I 2 [GGM II 471]); Eudoxos preferred 2 : 1 (fr. 276a Lasserre = Agathem. I 2 [GGM II 471]); Dikaiarchos chose 3 : 2 (fr. 109 Wehrli = Agathem. I 2 [GGM II 471]); Aristotle estimated by means of *periploi* and *itineraria* that the ratio was "more than 5 : 3" (meteor. II 5, p. 362b).

virtue of equator, poles and tropics in *About the measurement of the earth,* this was not the case with the parallel circles and meridians. Unlike modern geographers, Eratosthenes was incapable of determining more than a handful of parallel circles, and even less of the meridians. He did not try to produce a tight set of co-ordinates, therefore, but limited himself to mentioning only a few. According to Strabo, there was a total of seven parallels:

> This parallel [through the Cinnamon-producing country] passes outside the oikoumene, running, on the one side to the south of Taprobane or else to its furthermost inhabitants, and on the other side to the most southerly regions of Libya. (...) And the parallel through Meroe passes, on the one side through unknown regions, and on the other through the [southern] capes of India. (...) And the parallel through Syene passes, on the one side through the country of the Ichthyophagoi in Gedrosia and through India, and on the other through the regions that are almost 5,000 stades south of Cyrene. (...) And this parallel [through Alexandria] passes, on the one side through Cyrene and the regions 900 stades south of Carthage and central Maurusia, and on the other through Egypt, Coele Syria, Upper Syria, Babylonia, Susiana, Persia, Carmania, Upper Gedrosia, and India. (...) And according to Eratosthenes, this parallel [through Rhodes] runs through Caria, Lycaonia, Cataonia, Media, the Caspian Gates, and the parts of India along the Caucasus. (...) And a little north of it lies the parallel through Lysimachia, which, says Eratosthenes, passes through Mysia, Paphlagonia, Sinope, and the regions thereabouts, Hyrcania, and Bactra   (Strabo II 5, 35-40 C 133-34).

We can also derive Eratosthenes' meridians from the work of Strabo. The river Indus formed the first one. The second was located at the Caspian Gates and passed through the opening of the Persian Gulf to the Indian Ocean. The third ran through Thapsakos, a city on the Euphrates, whereas the fourth, the primary meridian, was laid through Alexandria and Rhodes, and a fifth through Carthage and Sicily.

Both the parallels and the meridians ran through some of the most notable cities of early Hellenistic times (Alexandria, Rhodes, Byzantion, Carthage etc.). They were chosen partly because of their significant status, and thus did not form a completely abstract and geometrical set of co-ordinates.[15] The meridians and parallel circles were determined not only by such places and the edges of the oikoumene, but also by natural boundaries like mountains, rivers and seas.

Eratosthenes was in fact the first geographer to draw parallel circles and meridians and develop them into a proper system.[16] By means of known distances and the fixing of points within his system of co-ordinates, it was now possible for him to construct a new map of the oikoumene. While his parallel circles and meridians do form a grid which resembles its modern cartographic counterpart, the truth is that his does not consist of infinite lines, nor does it have an astronomical basis.[17] Why did he bother to develop such a complicated and arbitrary framework at all? Part of the answer must be that he had only a limited set of data at his disposal (in addition to *periploi* and itineraries, perhaps tables of the maximum lengths of days, which he then converted into latitudes; his meridians recall ancient shipping routes).[18] In addition, the meridians and parallel circles served not only to determine the edges and periphery of the oikoumene, but also to divide it into smaller parts. In this connection it is puzzling that Eratosthenes gave up the ancient concept of the three continents (Europe, Asia, Africa). He deliberately rejected his predecessors' fruitless attempts to demarcate them by rivers or isthmoi.[19] In his opinion, these attempts had failed to produce convincing results, and in any case had been made redundant by recent

---

[15] F. Prontera, 'Sulle basi empiriche della cartografia greca', in: *Sileno* 23, 1997, 49-63.

[16] In one passage Strabo (II 5, 16 C 120) called the meridians and parallel circles "elements" (στοιχεῖα), here presumably citing Eratosthenes. Cf. Berger op. cit. 222.

[17] There were two different kinds of meridians and parallel circles. Eratosthenes considered the meridian running from Syene to Alexandria as the main one, and extended it to Rhodes, the Hellespont and the mouth of the river Borysthenes.

[18] Prontera op. cit.

[19] The controversy over the term ἤπειρος is ably discussed by K. Zimmermann, *Libyen: Das Land südlich des Mittelmeers im Weltbild der Griechen*, Munich 1999, 24-36.

discoveries. He therefore felt compelled to develop a new concept of division and to match it to his map.

From Strabo (II 1, 22-39 C 78-92) we gather that he divided the oikoumene into a northern and a southern "division" (βόρειον/νώτιον μέρος, not to be confused with hemispheres). At parallel 36° N he drew a line from the Pillars of Hercules to the Taurus mountains and beyond as far as the most distant points of Asia, by taking over a feature developed by Aristotle's pupil Dikaiarchos of Messene[20] and later termed (presumably by Eratosthenes himself) "diaphragma".[21]

Having divided the oikoumene into these two major divisions, Eratosthenes was prompted to subdivide them in turn into irregular sections termed *sphragides* ("seals"):

> As part of his idea already mentioned about the Taurus range and the Mediterranean beginning at the Pillars, Eratosthenes divides the oikoumene by means of this line into two divisions, and calls them the northern and southern respectively (βόρειον/νώτιον μέρος), and then attempts to cut each of these divisions again into such sections as are possible; and he calls these sections "seals" (σφραγῖδες).   (Strabo II 1, 22 C 78)

From Wilcken onwards, scholars have often reckoned[22] that Eratosthenes derived this term from the Ptolemaic land administration, where "seal" was synonymous with "parcel", i.e. an area of land marked off by cornerstones.[23] But there is no conclusive evidence that

---

[20] Agathem. 5 [GGM II 472] = fr. 110 Wehrli = fr. 123 Mirhady; cf. Strabo II 1, 1 C 67-8.

[21] The noun "diaphragma" (διάφραγμα) is derived from the verb διαφράγνυμι, "to barricade". The term is not attested for Dikaiarchos (he spoke of a τομὴ εὐθεῖα εὔκρατος), so possibly it was coined by Eratosthenes.

[22] U. Wilcken, *Griechische Ostraka aus Aegypten und Nubien*, vol. I, Leipzig and Berlin 1899, 210 n. 1; cf. W. Kubitschek, 'Karten', in: *Paulys Realencyclopädie der classischen Altertumswissenschaft*, vol. X 2, Stuttgart 1919, 2022-2149 at 2053-4; Geus op. cit. 276.

[23] F. Preisigke, *Fachwörterbuch des öffentlichen Verwaltungsdienstes Ägyptens in den griechischen Papyrusurkunden der ptolemäisch-römischen Zeit*, Göttingen 1915 (repr. 1975), 166. If I am not mistaken, the earliest attestations of σφραγίς

"seal" was used in this sense before the publication of Eratosthenes' *Geographika*.[24] My guess would be that Eratosthenes was thinking of the impression in wax made by a signet ring.[25] Geographically speaking, a "seal" is to be regarded as a region marked by distinctive lines and landmarks. Strabo, who is our sole source for the term, also speaks of μέρη, μερίδες and πλίνθια (of which at least πλίνθιον has a geometrical significance).[26]

Since this system of subdivision devised by Eratosthenes found little favour with later geographical writers, our grasp of it is unavoidably limited. At least we know that his description of "seals" started in south-east Asia. The first and greatest of them comprised India. He called it ῥομβοειδής ("rhomboidal"), i.e. a four-sided figure with only the opposite sides and angles being equal.

India is bounded on the north, from Ariana to the eastern sea, by the extremities of the Taurus (…); on the west by the Indus river; but the southern and eastern sides, which are much greater than the other two, extend into the Atlantic sea, and thus the shape of the country becomes rhomboidal, each of the greater sides exceeding the opposite side by as much as 3,000 stades …   (Strabo XV 1, 11 C 689; cf. II 1, 22 C 78)

This passage confirms that the first "seal" is not in fact a true rhomboid, since its opposite sides are said not to be equal (cf. fig. 3). To the first "seal" a second is added, comprising Ariane, bordered to the west in form of a parallelogram (παραλληλόγραμμον σχῆμα). Again, Strabo cites Eratosthenes:

Eratosthenes says that Ariana is bounded on the east by the Indus river, on the south by the Great Sea, on the north by the Paropamisos mountain

---

or σφραγῖδες are UPZ 1928, 4 (244 [or 219/18?] BC, but the exact meaning is unclear), and BGU XIV 2385, 3 (c. 214-12 BC).

[24] For its publication date (last two decades of the 3rd century BC), see Geus op. cit. 284-5.

[25] Cf. Berger op. cit. 223-4.

[26] For πλίνθιον ("rectangle" or "square") see Berger op. cit. 223, n. 2.

and the mountains that follow it as far as the Caspian Gates, and that its parts on the west are marked by the same boundaries by which Parthia is separated from Media and Carmania from Paraitakene and Persis.

(Strabo XV 2, 8 C 723)

Although he [Eratosthenes] sees that it [Ariana] has at least three sides well-suited to the formation of the figure of a parallelogram, and although he cannot mark off the western side by exact points, as the tribes there alternate with one another, yet he represents that side by a sort of line that begins at the Caspian Gates and ends at the capes of Carmania that are next to the Persian Gulf (...) And so, though he represents the second "seal" merely by a rough outline [ὁλοσχειρεῖ τινι τύπῳ], he represents the third "seal" much more roughly than the second – and for several reasons.

(Strabo II 1, 22-3 C 78)

Strabo at once proceeds to elaborate upon why the third "seal" is "much more roughly" represented:

First is the reason already mentioned, namely, because the side beginning at the Caspian Gates and running to Carmania (the side common to the second and third "seals") has not been determined distinctly; secondly, because the Persian Gulf breaks into the southern side – as Eratosthenes himself says, and therefore he has been forced to take the line beginning at Babylon as though it were a straight line running through Susa and Persepolis to the frontiers of Carmania and Persis, on which he was able to find a measured highway, which was slightly more than 9,000 stades long all told. This side Eratosthenes calls "southern", but he does not call it parallel to the northern side. Again, it is clear that the Euphrates, by which he marks off the western side, is nowhere near a straight line; but after flowing from the mountains towards the south, it then turns eastward, and then southward again to the point where it empties into the sea. And Eratosthenes makes clear the river's lack of straightness when he indicates the shape of Mesopotamia, which results from the confluence of the Tigris and the Euphrates – "like a galley", as he says. And besides, as regards the stretch from Thapsakos to Armenia, Eratosthenes does not even have measurements to cover the entire western side that is marked off by the Euphrates; in fact, he says he does not know the extent of the stretch next to Armenia and the northern mountains because it is unmeasured. For all these reasons, therefore, he says he represents the third "seal" only in rough outline (τυπωδῶς); indeed, he says that he collected even the distances from many writers who had worked out the itineraries – some of which he speaks of as actually untitled. (Strabo II 1, 23 C 78-9)

The exceptional difficulty of determining the third "seal" is clear. For its uneven southern side broken by the Persian Gulf, Eratosthenes only had access to the survey of the route stretching from Babylonia through Susa and Persepolis to the frontiers of Carmania. The western side – represented by the Euphrates – did not consist of a straight line; nor was the northern border running from the Caspian Gates to the Euphrates parallel to the mountain range either.

While the first and second "seals" represent single territories (India and Ariana), this was not true of the third. Eratosthenes evidently paid little attention to political boundaries. Rather, his division was neither "traditional" nor "organic", since he ignored the ancient concept of the continents and conceived lines which were imaginary. His first goal as a geographer was to divide the oikoumene into units whose corner points and borderlines could be measured or calculated with a certain precision. Consequently, he himself stated that the third "seal" was defined only "in rough outline" (τυπωδῶς, Strabo II 1, 23 C 79)[27]. The shape of the third "seal" is not stated explicitly, but the impression from Strabo must be that it was either a trapezium or a rhomboid.

To determine the fourth and smallest "seal", we have even fewer indicators. Strabo says that it enclosed the area between the Euphrates and the Mediterranean Sea, and extended south down to Arabia Felix. Since this means it comprised Arabia Felix and the Arabian Gulf, as well as all of Egypt and Ethiopia, it evidently overstepped the ancient boundary between the continents of Asia and Africa:

---

[27] τυπωδῶς means in the first place "like an outline" and refers to the impression of the "seal" (τύπωμα means "seal impression"). Thus, an accurate translation would not be "rough" or "uncertain", but rather "sketchy" or "outlined", i. e. only the edges and contours of the shape are clear.

Of this section, the length will be the space bounded by two meridian lines, one drawn through the westernmost point of the section and the other through the easternmost. Its breadth will be the space between two parallels of latitude, one drawn through the northernmost point, and the other through the southernmost; for in the case of irregular figures whose length and breadth it is impossible to determine by sides, we must determine their size in this way.   (Strabo II 1, 32 C 85; cf. II 1, 36 C 88)

We are not informed about any further "seals" beyond these four, but the assumption must be that Eratosthenes divided the entire oikoumene thus. It is very likely that all seals had a serial number. If the rest were more or less as large as the known ones, the total number of "seals" was presumably no more than a dozen or two.[28]

Strabo's account of the four "seals" indicates that Eratosthenes determined their outlines not only by a morphological break or measured distance (like a watershed or a route) but also by an "artificial" line (a meridian or parallel circle). A single feature might even serve both purposes; the Indus river, for example, which separated India and Ariana, also formed a meridian. Thus, the outlines of the "seals" were at least partly identical with the meridians and the parallel circles determined by Eratosthenes. If such imaginary lines could correspond to boundaries of lands and "seals", we may conclude that while the framework of Eratosthenes' map was more geographical or hodological than astronomical, even so his goal was not an organic division of the oikoumene but rather a geometric one.[29] Thus Eratosthenes could better determine, first the size of the inhabited world as a whole, and second the position, shape and size of its parts.

Strabo's account reveals that Eratosthenes used even smaller units than "seals". Mesopotamia, a part of the third "seal", is compared to a galley.[30] This kind of "shape" was no exception. Eratosthenes made use

---

[28] Cf. Berger op. cit. 19.
[29] Berger op. cit. 11 is fond of speaking of a "geometrische Methode" of Eratosthenes.
[30] Cf. II 1, 26 C 80; XVI 1, 22 C 746; Eust. comm. Dion. perieg. 976.

of other "shapes" to illustrate particular regions of his map:[31] He pictured Africa in the form of a right-angled triangle.[32] He took over from Hekataios of Miletos[33] the metaphor of the Scythian bow for the Pontos. He also compared the course of the Nile to the letter N.[34] Maybe, too, the strange comparison of the oikoumene with a *chlamys* can be traced back to him.[35] If he described the whole oikoumene in this manner – and we have no good reason to believe otherwise –, then it would be a fair guess that he is the source for all the "shapes" known from Strabo and other geographers (human head, cook's knife, oxhide, leaf of a plane-tree etc.).[36]

There is a didactic intention behind the "seals" and "shapes". Even if Eratosthenes' system was unable to reflect the actual conditions in detail, it nevertheless conveyed to his contemporaries an adequate image of the oikoumene and the relative size and position of its parts. It is more than likely that this representation of countries and landmasses by "seals" and "shapes" reinforced Eratosthenes' aim of constructing a clearly arranged and easy memorable map. From his data it should be easy to discern the outlines of the oikoumene and its parts, and even to reproduce his map. Accordingly, the map lacks certain features which we take for granted today (astronomical determination of essential corner points; correction of the distortion caused by the plane projection; accurate scale, etc.). In addition, the boundaries of countries are represented by straight lines and oriented only to the four cardinal points. Consequently, Eratosthenes' concern was that his map should be readily drawn, copied and memorized.

---

[31] Good overview in K. Brodersen, *Terra Cognita: Studien zur römischen Raumerfassung*, Hildesheim, Zurich, New York 1995 (²2003), 39-43 and 95-99.

[32] Strabo XVII 3, 1 C 825; cf. Zimmermann op. cit. 120-1.

[33] Amm. XXII 8, 9-14; cf. Sall fr. III 63 Maurenbrecher (from Serv. Aen. III 533); Mela I 102; Plin. NH IV 76; 86; Dionys. Per. 156-163; Avien. orb. terr. 224-242; Prisc. periheg. 146-152; Eust. comm. Dion. perieg. 157 (GGM II 245).

[34] Strabo XVII 1, 2 C 785-6.

[35] K. Zimmermann, 'Eratosthenes' chlamys-shaped world: a misunderstood metaphor', in: D. Ogden and A. Powell (eds), *The Hellenistic World: New Perspectives*, London 2003.

His procedure should not be regarded as making a complete breach with the geographical tradition. He followed both old and new directions. With all the "seals", as well as the "shapes", he managed to structure quantities of data and synthesize them successfully. By fully exploiting the information available from his sources, he established a solid enough basis for his map of the oikoumene, even if it fell short in detail. Certainly it was a major improvement on the older maps of the Ionian geographers, though it did still reflect the analogy, symmetry, and speculation that were such characteristic features of their efforts.

Eratosthenes' *Geographika* were dictated by insight and restraint. Viewed in this way, his geographical achievements may be seen to achieve a judicious compromise between the claims of theory on one side and practical feasibility on the other.[37]

---

[36] For the use of "shape" in ancient geography see Strabo II 1, 30 C 83-4, who is likely to be drawing upon Eratosthenes.

[37] Cf. Geus op. cit. 288.

Ptolemy and the Problem
of Scientific Perception of Space[*]

Alfred Stückelberger

1. Historical conditions

When, shortly after the middle of the 2nd century AD, Ptolemy started to present, as a pendant to his recently published astronomical work, the geographical knowledge of his times, he faced the almost impossible problem of combining the mass of readily available, but rather unreliable, data presented in itineraries, logs, road maps, reports on expeditions etc., with the few scientifically (i.e. astronomically) proven data available to him from which to create a coherent geographical view of the world.

Well before him Eratosthenes of Cyrene (276-194 BC) had begun to research solid foundations for a map of the world (which has not survived), which makes him the founding father of scientific geography. Once the shape of the earth as a globe had been discovered,[1] making the previous simple periplus maps obsolete,[2] it was necessary to acquire an idea of the size of the earth. Eratosthenes' calculations, which are known in detail, arrive at a circumference of 252,000 stades[3],

---

[*] I am grateful to Kai Brodersen for the translation of this paper.
[1] This idea, which seems to have been developed in the late 5th century BC in Pythagorean circles, seems to be referred to for the first time in Plat. Phaid. 110b; the earliest conclusive piece of evidence is the observation of the projection of the earth's shadow at lunar eclipses in Aristot., met. 297b 24 sqq.
[2] Cf. Herodotus' criticism (4, 36, 2) of the circular periplus by Hecataeus of Miletus (ca. 500 BC).
[3] The method is known through Cleomedes, de motu circulari 1, 10, 3 sq.;

something between 39,700 km and 41,700 km, depending on the length of the stade used for the calculation;[4] this value was not improved upon until the 17th century.[5] Eratosthenes also started to use gnomon measurements and observing the length of the longest day[6] to identify "important cities" (πόλεις ἐπίσημοι) on the same latitude and relate them to the oikoumene's seven *klimata* which were to become canonical – preliminary work of the utmost importance for Ptolemy.[7]

Eratosthenes' endeavours were continued, with various corrections, by the astronomer Hipparchus of Nicaea (ca. 180-125 BC), who was known for his precise measurements, but failed to compile a geographical work of his own. His special achievement was that he discovered an ingenious method for identifying longitude – a task which is far more difficult than identifying latitude – by observing lunar eclipses; we shall return to it below.[8]

After these promising approaches to geodetical definitions, geographical literature (with the exception of Marinus of Tyre, Ptolemy's immediate predecessor) was mainly removed from mathematical observation and limited to ethnographical and topographical accounts, as in the fragments of Polybius (ca. 120 BC), in the large work of Strabo (early 1st century AD) and in the less ambitious Latin survey of Pomponius Mela (ca. AD 40).

With the vast expansion of the geographical horizon in the Hellenistic age and in the early Roman empire, the task of developing a

---

see further A. Stückelberger, *Einführung in die antiken Naturwissenschaften*, Darmstadt 1988, 187 sq. and Geus in this volume.

[4] It seems to me that the stade to be used for this calculation should take into account the distance of 5000 stades from Alexandria to Syene (Assuan), so the Egyptian stade of 157.5 m or the stade equalling one ninth of a mile or 165.4 m are the most likely candidates.

[5] In 1671, Jean Picard calculated a circumference of 20,541,600 toises (40,035 km).

[6] On these methods of measurement see below.

[7] See especially E. Honigmann, *Die sieben Klimata und die Poleis episemoi*, Heidelberg 1929, 10 sqq.

[8] Cf. Strabo 1, 1, 12; see below.

new integration of geographical data on a scientific foundation became even more urgent.

Northwards, already in ca. 330 BC Pytheas of Massalia had sailed beyond Britain and had written about a mysterious island called *Thule*, which henceforth was used to mark the northernmost extension of the oikoumene.[9] Further exact data had been acquired shortly before AD 84 when Agricola had sent a party to sail around Britain which had led to the discovery of the *Orcades Insulae*, the Orkney islands.[10] On the continent, the Romans had marched far into inner Germany; in AD 5 Tiberius had led an army as far as the Elbe[11], and at some later time the field of Roman vision had been extended as far as the Weichsel and the northern end of Denmark.[12]

Southwards, already in 148/7 BC the historian Polybius, using boats provided for this purpose by the younger Scipio, had followed the traces of Hanno in a voyage of discovery along the coastline of western Africa[13]. Towards the south-east, around 25 BC, Aelius Gallus had marched as far as *Arabia Felix*,[14] while some time later an otherwise unknown Dioscorus had sailed along the eastern coast of Africa probably as far as the equator.[15] One individual had even got far into central

---

[9] Cf. Strabo 1, 4, 2. The violent criticism which Strabo and later authors direct against Pytheas' reports is hardly justified. Correct description of the midnight sun – a phenomenon which Strabo completely failed to explain – proves Pytheas' knowledge of some conditions in the polar region (cf. Cleom. de motu circ. 1, 7).

[10] Cf. Tac. Agric. 10, 5.

[11] Cf. Vell. Pat. 2, 106, 2.

[12] Cf. Plin. nat. hist. 4, 81.97.

[13] Cf. Plin. nat. hist. 5, 9; the exact time of this voyage cannot be defined. Already in the 5th century BC the Carthaginian sailor Hanno had travelled as far as the gulf of Guinea; his report is preserved in a Greek version (GGM 1, 1-14).

[14] Cf. Strabo 16, 4, 22; Plin. nat. hist. 6, 160.

[15] Cf. Ptol. geogr. 1, 9, 3 sqq. and 4, 8, 2 (here, and elsewhere, I quote from Nobbe's edition, on which see below). Ptolemy identifies the southern terminus of this voyage, the *Prasum promonturium*, at 15° southern latitude and thus too far south.

Africa: around 23/22 BC Petronius, fighting against the Nubian queen
Candace, had followed the course of the Nile as far as *Napata* on the
fourth cataract.[16] Nero had measured the distance to the Nubian capital *Meroe* which was situated even further to the south.[17] Even the
sources of the Nile – Pliny specifically mentions a 'lake' – seem at least
to have been known from hearsay.[18] Under Domitian the Roman general Iulius Maternus, starting from *Leptis Magna* in Libya, had marched
for four months into central Africa as far as *Agisymba*.[19]

As for the far east, a certain view even of China and Tibet had been
acquired among the regions beyond India (which had been quite well
known ever since Alexander's conquests) thanks to the active trade
along the silk route.[20]

2. The theoretical foundations of a new image of the *oikoumene*[21]

The enormous increase in the knowledge of frequently unrelated
and often credible detailed data (which could not, however, be used
immediately for geodesy) had to be processed and brought into a
coherent framework. Marinus of Tyre (ca. AD 80-130), in a work with
the self-confident title "Correction of the geographical map"[22], had
started to tackle this task and transfer this data onto a map of the
world. He had used quite arbitrary conversions of the figures in itinera-

---

[16] Strabo 17, 1, 54; Plin. nat. hist. 6, 181 sq.
[17] Plin. nat. hist. 6, 184.
[18] Plin. nat. hist. 5, 51.
[19] Ptol. geogr. 1, 8, 4 sqq., around the region of Lake Chad.
[20] Cf. below note 48.
[21] For the whole complex of questions cf. A. Stückelberger, 'Die geographi-
      sche Ortsbestimmung und das Problem der synchronen Zeitmessung',
      Études de Lettres: Revue de la faculté des lettres, Université Lausanne 1986, 54 sqq.
      185-195 and id., loc. cit. 54 sqq.; a good account now in J.L. Berggren &
      A. Jones, *Ptolemy's Geography: An annotated translation of the theoretical chapters,*
      Princeton 2000, esp. 23-41.
[22] Ptol. geogr. 1, 6, 1: τοῦ γεωγραφικοῦ πίνακος διόρθωσις.

ries to try and gain reliable data, but in the process had become entangled in many contradictions – as Ptolemy had pointed out critically.[23] The work seems to have remained unfinished.[24]

Not long afterwards Ptolemy (Claudius Ptolemaius of Alexandria, ca. AD 100-180) undertook to tackle the same task and gathered the complete geographical knowledge of his times in a copious work entitled "Handbook of Geography" (ὑφήγησις γεωγραφική) and thus saved it for posterity. While this work is unique in its importance for the history of science, there is neither a recent edition nor a modern translation of the whole text. The only complete edition, by Carl Friedrich August Nobbe, appeared in 1843-1845 and has repeatedly been reprinted; later projects have remained unfinished.[25] Now the "Ptolemaios-Forschungsstelle" in Bern has made a fresh start. As a collaborative effort by scholars from a variety of countries, it aims to publish a new edition with a (German) translation and integrated maps.[26] The Greek text will be based on fresh collation of a few primary manuscripts (with other codices used in individual cases); the maps are to be drawn according to Ptolemy's instructions. The whole edition is designed to be user-friendly and, thanks to a modern translation, accessible to a wider audience.

Shortly before AD 150 Ptolemy had presented the astronomical knowledge of his time in a work which is known under its later Arabic-

---

[23] Cf. the detailed criticism of Marinus in Ptol. geogr. 1, 6ff. (incidentally, this is nearly our only source for Marinus).

[24] Cf. Ptol. geogr. 1, 17, 1.

[25] The edition by Carl Müller (Paris 1883-1901) only presents books 1-5, while Paul Schnabel sadly could not bring his project to publication at all.

[26] It is a pleasure to use this opportunity to mention the scholars currently engaged in the project: Renate Burri (Bern), Robert Fuchs (Köln), Klaus Geus (Bamberg), Franco Giorgianni (Palermo), Gerd Grasshoff (Bern; joint project leader), Wolfgang Hübner (Münster), Helmut Humbach (Mainz), Kurt Keller (Thun), Lutz Koch (Hamburg), Florian Mittenhuber (Bern), Heinz-Günther Nesselrath (Göttingen), Neel Smith (Worcester, USA), Alfred Stückelberger (Bern; joint project leader), Gerhard Winkler (Linz) and Susanne Ziegler (Darmstadt).

Greek title "Almagest". In structure it is comparable to the geographical work: theoretical discussion, followed by a catalogue of fixed stars combined with an atlas of constellations.[27] Here already Ptolemy announces his geographical work:

> It remains only to ascertain the geographical position of the major cities of every province according to their longitude and latitude. ... We shall publish the table with the relevant data in a separate geographical work. ... This index is to contain the necessary data on how many degrees every individual city is away from the equator on the meridian it is crossed by, and how many degrees this meridian is away from the one crossing Alexandria towards the east or the west on the equator.   (Ptolemy, Almagest 2, 13)

In this notice Ptolemy outlines the basic concept which he was to realize in his "Handbook of Geography". For the first time, the locations of places were to be presented in a uniform system of coordinates with details of the degrees, abolishing the complicated recalculations of the lengths of shadows and days. The only later change was to transfer the meridian (which here crosses Alexandria) to the westernmost margin of the oikoumene at the *Insulae Fortunatae*. The basic presupposition for the demanding recalculations of the lengths of shadows into degrees had been created by Ptolemy in his table of chords presented in Almagest 1, 11, where the lengths of the chords for the angles from 0° to 180° are presented in intervals of half a degree (cf. fig. 4).[28]

---

[27] Traces of this atlas are preserved in the transmission of Aratus and in the Arabic transmission of As-sufi; cf. A. Stückelberger, "Sterngloben und Sternkarten: Zur wissenschaftlichen Bedeutung des Leidener Aratus", *Museum Helveticum* 47, 1990, 70-81.

[28] With this table it is possible to use the length of the shadow of a gnomon to find out the latitude φ and the length of the longitudinal degree: the shadow can be considered as the chord of φ. – As an example for the precision of the values thus acquired we can look at the chord for an angle of 90°, which is equal to $\sqrt{2}$; recalculating from the hexagesimal system into a decimal system, one arrives at 1.414212 (the true value is 1.414213).

As Ptolemy put it in the first chapters of his theoretical introduction, when drawing maps, one had to start from astronomically fixed points serving, as it were, as foundations (θεμέλιοι).[29] To identify the geographical latitude there were two methods available: (a) measuring the length of the shadow cast by a gnomon (the ὄργανον σκιόθηρον) on the equinox (the relation of the length of the shadow to the height of the gnomon is equivalent to the tangent of the polar height or the geographical latitude φ; cf. fig. 5). This method had been known for a long time before Ptolemy: Pytheas of Massalia, in the later 4th century BC, had already used gnomon measurements to compare the latitudes of Massalia and Byzantium.[30] Vitruvius relates that complete lists of such "lengths of shadows" had been compiled[31] and presents some results which allow us an impression of the precision achieved with these measurements (which coincide well with the data in the catalogue of places in Ptolemy).[32]

	Relation of length of shadow to height of gnomon (tang φ) acc. to Vitr.	*= latitude according to Vitr.*	*Values in Ptolemy's catalogue of places*	*actual values*
Rome	8/9 = 0.888	41° 40' N	41° 40' N	41° 55' N
Athens	3/4 = 0.750	36° 50' N	37° 15' N	37° 55' N
Rhodes	5/7 = 0.714	35° 35' N	36° 0' N	36° 20' N
Tarentum	9/11 = 0.818	39° 20' N	40° 0' N	40° 25' N
Alexandria	3/5 = 0.600	31° 0' N	31° 0' N	31° 15' N

[29] Ptol. geogr. 1, 4, 2.
[30] Cf. Strabo 1, 4, 4.
[31] Vitr. 9, 7, 1; similar values in Plin. nat. hist. 6, 212 sqq.
[32] Considering that gnomon measurements are marred by a systematical error of −16' (that is half the diameter of the sun) – since the shadow is not defined by the centre, but by the upper margin of the sun –, the precision is indeed astonishing (and invalidates the criticism of Berggren & Jones

(b) The geographical latitude could be calculated very precisely from the length of the longest day, as this day's duration increases continually from the equator to the polar circle. This method of calculation had been explained by Ptolemy in Almagest 2, 3. In Geography 1, 23, in the instructions on how to draw a map of the world, he presents a list of 21 latitudes with the respective lengths of their days:

length of day on summer solstice (hours)	*= latitude acc. to Ptol. geogr. 1, 23*	*calculated values*
12	0°	0°
12,5	8° 25' N	8° 25' 18" N
13	16° 25' N	16° 27' 40" N
13,5	23° 50' N	23° 49' 40" N etc.
20	63° 0' N	62° 58' 28" N

The astronomical calculation of longitude, however, proved to be far more difficult – a fact known to Ptolemy:

> Most distances, however, and especially those towards East or West, are transmitted rather imprecisely, not because of a lack of seriousness on the relevant scholars' part, but rather because of the fact that a calculation based on astronomical observation had not been widely used, nor had attention been given to lunar eclipses observed at the same time in different places, like the one which happened in Arbela at the 5th hour, but in Carthage at the 2nd.[33] Such attention could in fact result in a knowledge of the distance between two places, in equatorial degrees, towards East or West.[34]   (Ptol. geogr. 1, 4, 2)

loc. cit. 29).

[33] On this eclipse see below.

[34] This method is already hinted at in Almagest 2, 1; cf. also Theo Smyrn. p. 121, 1 Hill.

Thus the method of calculating longitude is sketched out; it seems to go back to Hipparchus.[35] Lacking instruments for measuring (independently of the sun) the time at which various celestial bodies crossed the meridian, Hipparchus had the brilliant idea of making use of lunar eclipses for this purpose. As the time at which the moon passes into the earth's shadow is nearly identical for all places on earth, but occurs at different moments depending on the local time, this could be used for finding out longitudes, since a difference of one hour is equal to 15 degrees in longitude (cf. fig. 6).[36]

Hence the methods of how to state the geographical coordinates for any place had been invented, at least in theory. All that remained to do was to state the method by which the many places were to be marked on the map. Ptolemy devised a new method of projection for a map of the world which cannot be discussed here[37]; he also drafted the outlines of 26 regional maps to which he relates the ca. 8000 places mentioned in his catalogue of places in the oikoumene. The problem in devising these maps was to deal with the 'shortening' of longitudinal degrees from the equator to the poles (since the earth is spherical) so as not to suffer excessive distortions. For these regional maps – unlike the one of the world – he decided to use a rectangular cylindrical projection, with the central parallel circle of the individual map dictating the length of the longitudinal degrees. Book 8 presents for every map the so-called 'factor of shortening', that is the relation of longitude in the centre of the map to the equator, which is identical with the cos φ (cf. fig. 7). To illustrate the precision of this calculation here are some values given in this context:

---

[35] Cf. Strabo 1, 1, 12.
[36] See further below.
[37] Ptol. geogr. 1, 24; cf. Berggren & Jones and Stückelberger locc. citt.

map	'shortening factor' of the central circle in book 8	$\cos \varphi$ of the central parallel circle (calculated)
Europe 1 (geogr. 8,3)	11/20 (0.55)	$\cos 57° = 0.5445$
Europe 2 (geogr. 8,4)	3/4 (0.75)	$\cos 41° = 0.754$
Africa 1 (geogr. 8,14)	13/14 (0.866)	$\cos 30° = 0.866$
Africa 2 (geogr. 8,19)	11/15 (0.733)	$\cos 43° = 0.731$

3. The problem of practical realization

Ptolemy's coherent model allows all components to be checked mathematically and continues to influence the shape of maps down to the present day with the concepts of longitude and latitude, with the arc of 360 degrees (the only modern change being the transfer of the "zero-meridian" from the *Insulae Fortunatae* to Greenwich), and with placing north at the top. The problem Ptolemy could not solve, however, was the fact that he could only muster very few astronomical data defined by using this method. Well before him, a catalogue of "important cities" (πόλεις ἐπίσημοι) had been started to serve as a basic pattern for developing maps.[38] Ptolemy names some 360 of these cities in book 8, but not even all of them had been defined astronomically. Instead, they had been attributed to the seven *klimata* according to the methods just explained[39], and quite reliable data for their latitudes had been achieved – unlike for the longitudes, which were defined using the very rare lunar eclipses, as Ptolemy himself admits.[40] The lunar eclipse he cites in the quotation above is the one which Alexander the Great witnessed during his march on September 20th, 331 BC at Arbela not far from the Tigris. It had begun – as

---

[38] On this see Honigmann loc. cit. 58 sqq.
[39] Cf. Honigmann loc. cit. 10 sqq.
[40] Cf. Ptol. geogr. 1, 4, 2 (quoted above).

modern calculations have proved[41] – at 19.33 MET. According to Ptolemy it had happened three hours earlier at Carthage than in Arbela. The data he had to rely on were rather imprecise, as the real time difference between Arbela (2 hours and 55 minutes east) and Carthage (0 hours and 41 minutes east) is only 2 hours and 14 minutes, but the problem lies with the positions given by Ptolemy for the location of these places: Carthage at 34° 50' (in geogr. 4, 3, 2) and Arbela at 80° (in geogr. 6, 1, 5) – thus claiming an unduly large distance between the two of 45° 10' (or 3 hours and ⅔ minutes).[42] In Almagest 5, 14, however, Ptolemy presents more exact data for the time differences when lunar eclipses are observed. The eclipse of April 22nd, 621 BC started at Babylon 5 hours and 50 minutes past midnight and at Alexandria 5 hours past midnight, which makes the longitudinal distance 50 minutes or 12° 30' (in fact, it is 58 minutes or 14° 30'). Both examples illustrate how far back Ptolemy had to go in order to find – apparently by chance – information of this kind.

The 'overstretching' of longitudes affects all of Ptolemy's geographical work. Even a brief glimpse at his map of the world shows an oikoumene which is stretched out too much; according to Ptolemy the oikoumene, from the *Insulae Fortunatae* to the (as yet unlocated) 'metropolis' Sinai in Eastern China, covers 180° of the circumference of the globe.[43] In the regional maps the same 'overstretching' is noticeable and leads, for instance, to the rather 'flat' position of Italy in the Mediterranean. To be sure, one should acknowledge that Ptolemy's 180° are a striking reduction of the value given by Marinus, who had postulated 15 hours or 225°.[44] Justifying this reduction, Ptolemy remarkably refers to the astronomical argument, according to which observations of lunar eclipses are never further apart than 12 hours.[45]

---

[41] Cf. S.F.K. Ginzel, *Spezieller Kanon der Sonnen- und Mondfinsternisse für das Ländergebiet der klassischen Altertumswissenschaften*, Berlin 1899.

[42] Observations of the same lunar eclipse are also referred to in Pliny, nat. hist. 2, 180.

[43] In fact, it is only some 144° from the Cape Verde Islands to Shanghai.

[44] Cf. Ptol. geogr. 1, 11, 1.

[45] Ptol. synt. 2, 1 p. 88 Heib.

For the regions in the Far East and south of the equator, astronomical data were lacking even for the πόλεις ἐπίσημοι. Thus, to arrive at the coordinates for the other nearly 8000 places in his catalogue Ptolemy was forced to use other, less reliable methods. The collections of data available to him seem to have included lists compiled by predecessors like Marinus of Tyre, by the Roman provincial administration (probably including files going back to Ptolemaic times), and more recent itineraries and descriptions of sea routes etc. These sources, which provide a wealth of interesting detail on trade routes, borders of districts, government administration and so on, still await further research. At least some details are known. Thus Ptolemy had access not only to the material he takes from Marinus, but also to an – albeit incomplete – list of *coloniae* and legionary bases[46] which must go back to the provincial administration.

Another source which was available through Marinus is even referred to by name: a "measuring of ways" (ἀναμήτρησις) of the Macedonian trader Maës Tatianus[47], who – without having been there in person – seems to have related what he had heard from the leaders of caravans about the trade route from the Mediterranean via the "Stone Tower" to Sera (in China)[48] – obviously a reference to the famous Silk Route.[49] Ptolemy's detailed discussion here illustrates how difficult, even impossible, it was to arrive at reliable coordinates from such an itinerary which presented distances in "days of travel", especially given the natural bends in a route and the lack of data on its orientation. To try and deduct a certain amount from the overall dis-

---

[46] In Book 2 (on Britain, Gaul and Pannnonia) he refers to 11 legionary bases, in Book 3 (Moesia) to 3 and in Book 4 to 1.

[47] He is otherwise unknown and may have lived around 100 BC.

[48] Ptol. geogr. 1, 11, 7. – Sera, which must have been the terminus of the Silk Route, may possibly be identified with Lanzhou (Liang-Chou), the "Stone Tower" perhaps with Kashgar. In any case silk is attested in Rome from the time of Augustus, and was called *serica* long before Ptolemy. Cf. L. Bounois, *La Route de la Soie*, Vienna 1964.

[49] Cf. Berggren & Jones loc. cit. 150-152.

tance to account for bends in the road, and to calculate an "oblique" orientation trigonometrically into a distance on the meridian or the parallel circle, necessarily leads to unreliable results.

To trace the sources used by Ptolemy, special interest attaches to cases in which complete and coherent groups of places are systematically mislocated and thus bear no relation to geographical reality; this has recently been demonstrated by Claude Rapin.[50] In the data given for the regions of Margiana (geogr. 6, 10), Bactria (6, 11), and Sogdiana (6, 12), several places and rivers – of which some at least can be identified by their names and demonstrate a rather detailed knowledge of these remote regions – are shifted or inverted. Rapin suggests that several different regional maps with imprecise labels and variant orientations and scales had been used. They might even go back to the Seleucid administration and were, as Rapin plausibly argues, later put together wrongly, which led to the curious data in Ptolemy.[51] A similar observation can be made for the Alpine regions where, for instance, the region about Lake Geneva is shifted into the Tyrol.[52] Other errors are due to a mixing-up of names, to dittographies or wrong names, especially for names of peoples which were often put in a vacant space on a map, as has recently been demonstrated by H. Humbach and S. Ziegler.[53] It goes without saying that such errors occur mainly in regions outside the Roman Empire.

These examples may suffice to illustrate Ptolemy's dilemma: eager to practice the principles of scientific geography, he was obstructed by

[50] Cl. Rapin, 'L'incomprehensible Asie centrale de la carte de Ptolémée: Propositions pour un décodage', *Bulletin of the Asia Institute* 12, 1998 (2001), 201-225.

[51] Rapin, loc. cit., cites examples where a turning of individual segments by 45° to 180° produces results which are close to geographical reality.

[52] Cf. Ptol. geogr. 2, 12, 6 (this refers especially to the places *Octodurum* and *Eb<ur>odurum*.

[53] H. Humbach & S. Ziegler, *Ptolemy, Geography, Book 6, Middle East, Central and North Asia, China, Part 2,* in collaboration with K. Faiss; Maps in Simplified Reconstruction, Notes and Index, Wiesbaden 2002.

the practical problems of doing so when "unscientific" sources had to be used. This mismatch between scientific exactitude and source-related unreliabilty is clearly evident in his Geography. If one disregards these historical connections and proceeds on the basis of detailed modern knowledge, it is easy to list the many errors and problems in Ptolemy's Geography, and then to regard him as a second-rate compiler or even as a charlatan.[54] But historical context is vital. In this light, Ptolemy with his scientific approach, his array of data, and a structure of exemplary clarity, can be seen to have created a masterpiece which surpassed all his predecessors. It remained, when compared with late antique compendia or medieval circular maps, unsurpassed until the age of Columbus.[55]

[54] The most radical criticism, aimed in the first instance at Ptolemy's astronomical studies, but compromising Ptolemy the scientist altogether, has been launched by R.R. Newton, *The Crime of Claudius Ptolemy* (Baltimore 1977); most of his views, however, have been demolished by G. Grasshoff, *The History of Ptolemy's Star Catalogue* (New York and Berlin 1990).

[55] It may be noticed in passing that Columbus owned a copy of the Latin edition of the Geography ("Cosmographia", Rome 1478) and that he added notes especially to the data on the circumference of the earth; cf. A. Stückelberger , 'Kolumbus und die antiken Wissenschaften', *Archiv für Kulturgeschichte* 69, 1987, 331-340.

Roman Itinerary Literature

Sea and River Travel in the Roman Itinerary Literature[*]

Benet Salway

No tradition of navigational charts for plotting routes by sea or navigable rivers, such as the portolans of the Middle Ages, survives from Roman antiquity and it is doubtful that Roman sailors possessed such aids.[1] Those records of, or plans for, real journeys by water that are preserved survive largely in the form of purely verbal descriptions of routes. It is this itinerary literature that is the subject of this paper. My general purpose is to attempt to reconstruct something of the context in which this literature was produced (and in which it was later circulated and preserved) and to relate the forms it took to the contemporary experience of water-borne travel and the needs of travellers. The category 'Roman itinerary literature' is here taken to include not only works in Latin but also those by Greek authors writing under Roman hegemony, whether these writers were Roman citizens or not. Indeed, to overlook the hellenophone contribution would give rise to a very lopsided consideration of the subject. It may be a crude caricature to consider the Greeks as masters of the sea and the Romans as masters of the land, but the stereotype is confirmed by their respective domination of the technical vocabulary. The point is clear in reference

---

[*] Without suggesting their endorsement of the conclusions, thanks are due to S.J.J. Corcoran, P. Salway, R.J.A. Talbert, K.A Whitby, and participants in the conference session for discussions and comments that have improved the argument of this paper. All translations, unless otherwise indicated, are my own.

[1] G. Uggeri, "Portolani romani e carte nautiche: problemi e incognite" in G. Laudizi & C. Marangio (edd.), *Porti, approdi e linee di rotta nel Mediterraneo antico: Atti Seminario Studi, Lecce 1996* (Studi di Filologia e Letteratura 4, Galatina 1998) 31-78, argues a vigorous and detailed case for the existence of navigational charts, but the evidence remains slight and ambiguous.

to units of measurement. While Roman surveyors successfully exported the mile (*mille passuum*) wherever they laid out and built roads, the Greek stade (στάδιον) remained the normal unit for measuring travel by sea throughout the imperial period, in Latin as well as Greek texts. The surviving Latin and Greek sources for this topic do, in fact, complement each other very neatly, with very little overlap; this fact in itself may be significant and the pattern of the surviving itinerary collections will be examined in the light of the likely intentions of compilers and interests of users.

The bulk of maritime itineraries surviving from the Roman period is made up of the *Periplus maris interni* (*Circumnavigation of the Inner Sea*) by Menippus of Pergamum dating from the triumviral or very early Augustan period, the possibly almost contemporary but anonymous *Stadiasmus* or *Periplus maris magni* (*Measurement* or *Circumnavigation of the Great Sea*), and the anonymous *Periplus of the Red Sea*, of between AD 40 and 70, all in Greek.[2] Given its more exotic subject matter (the trade route to India), the last has attracted by far the most attention. Both for this reason and the fact that its topic lies largely outside the range of sea travel within the Roman world, of the Greek-language texts I shall be leaving aside the *Periplus of the Red Sea* and concentrating on the other two. The Latin itinerary tradition, on the other hand, is dominated by the so-called *Itinerarium Antonini*, an anonymous compilation dating from the late third century AD or later, but this is significantly supplemented by the graphic itinerary collection known as the *Tabula Peutingeriana* of uncertain date but, in its current form, no earlier than the second half of the fourth century.[3] These works exhibit a common

---

[2] The remains of Menippus' *Periplus* are edited by A. Diller, *The Tradition of the Minor Greek Geographers* (APA Monographs 14, Philadelphia 1952) 147-164; the most recent critical edition of the *Stadiasmus* is that in A. Bauer, *Hippolytus Werke* IV: *Die Chronik*, 2nd ed. rev. R.W.O. Helm (Die Griechischen christlichen Schriftsteller der ersten drei Jahrhunderte 46, Berlin 1955) sect. IV.9, 43-69; and that of the *Periplus of the Red Sea* is L. Casson, *The Periplus Maris Erythraei* (Princeton 1989), with arguments for dating at p.7.

[3] The standard critical edition of the *Itinerarium Antonini* is the Teubner edition by O. Cuntz, *Itineraria Romana* vol. I: *Itinerarium Antonini Augusti et*

utility as practical handbooks for the traveller planning a journey. This distinguishes them from both 'travel' literature, i.e. reports of specific journeys (whether documentary or literary prose, or poetry), on the one hand, and geographical treatises on the other (again, whether technical or literary prose, or poetry). Thus, under the heading of 'travel' literature can be categorised such things as the account of St. Paul's voyage to Rome in *Acts*, and Rutilius Claudius Namatianus' *De reditu suo*. Under 'geographical', along with the *Geography* of Ptolemy of Alexandria (Claudius Ptolemaeus), can be included the majority of the works making up the corpus of minor Greek geographers compiled by Marcianus of Heraclea Pontica in the fifth or early sixth-century AD,[4] as well as the tradition of verse guides (*periegeseis*) to the Mediterranean and Atlantic shores, most famously exemplified by that composed by one Dionysius in Alexandria under Hadrian.[5] Inevitably the various categories do shade into one another, especially given exploitation of geographers by *periplus*-writers and vice versa.[6] For instance, the *Periplus of the Black Sea* addressed by Flavius Arrianus (Arrian) to the emperor Hadrian c. AD 131/2 is a hybrid cross between a personal account of a single voyage and more general periegetic material.[7] More complex still, the author of the anonymous [Pseudo-Arrian] *Periplus of the Black Sea*

Burdigalense (Leipzig 1929), reprinted with updated bibliography by G. Wirth (Stuttgart 1990); that of the *Tabula Peutingeriana* by E. Weber, *Tabula Peutingeriana: Codex Vindobonensis 324. Kommentar / Vollständige Faksimil-Ausgabe im Originalformat* (Graz 1976); cf., however, Talbert in this volume.

[4] Diller, *Minor Greek Geographers* 45-46.

[5] O.A.W. Dilke, *Greek and Roman Maps* (London 1985) 143-44; this periegetic literature aimed to elucidate geography largely in relation to the Homeric epics. Dionysius was translated into Latin by both Rufus Festus Avienus and Priscianus, the former also imitating him in his own *Ora Maritima*.

[6] E.g. Marcianus of Heraclea heavily exploited Ptolemy's *Geography* to produce his *Periplus of the Outer Sea* (C. Müller, *Geographi Graeci Minores* vol. I [Paris 1854] 515-562), as did Dionysius for his *Periegesis*.

[7] A. Silberman, *Arrien, Périple du Pont-Euxin* (Collection Budé, Paris 1995) provides the most recent critical edition.

managed to blend Arrian and Menippus with historical and mythological information from the verse *periegesis* of Pausanias of Damascus [Pseudo-Scymnus], dedicated to king Nicomedes of Bithynia.[8] While reference will be made to works from these other categories in illustrating the real experience of travel and the way in which the itinerary literature relates to it, maintaining the distinctions is, nevertheless, a helpful tool for understanding the nature of their interrelationships.

1. Sea and River Travel in the Roman World

To put the itinerary literature into context, it is perhaps best to begin by considering the general nature and conditions of water-borne travel in antiquity. Its great advantage was of course speed. Marcianus of Heraclea provides some statistics on speeds of sea travel in his edition of Menippus' *Periplus* (on which more below). He reckons that the speed of an average ship with a favourable wind was 700 stades per day, reckoning the stade at 7.5 to the Roman mile (i.e. c. 70 nautical miles or 130 km per day, assuming a speed of 4.6 knots and a sailing day of 15 hours). For a fast ship he reckoned 900 stades per day and for a slow one 500.[9] This seems to accord with the testimony of the frequent international traveller and second-century orator, Aelius Aristides, who claimed, on the basis of personal experience, that a ship with a favourable wind could cover 1,200 stades in a single 24-hour period (a πανημερία) and certainly the large grain ships that did the Alexandria-Rome run and vice versa would keep sailing through day and night.[10] River travel had similar speed advantages – at least downstream – over its terrestrial counterpart, and even barges towed

---

[8] Anon., *Periplus Ponti Euxini* is edited by Diller, *Minor Greek Geographers* 102-146; Pausanias, *Periegesis ad Nicomedem regem* by Diller, op. cit. 165-176, with addendum p. 177 for identification of authorship.

[9] Marcianus, *Epitome* 5 (Müller, *GGM* I, 568), on which see P. Janni, *La mappa e il periplo: Cartografia antica e spazio odologico* (Università di Macerata, Pubblicazioni della Facoltà di Lettere e Filosofia 19, Rome 1984), 417.

[10] Aristides, *Or.* 48, 360 [605-610].

upstream had greater potential capacity than road-bound wagons. Two poems of Venantius Fortunatus afford us a vivid glimpse of the normality and scale of riverine peregrination by the Merovingian court in sixth-century Gaul.[11] It seems likely that this practice was inherited from their Roman predecessors. Still, it has been argued that the role of river transport in particular has been neglected by scholars and it has certainly had a low profile, even compared to sea travel, in discussions of the itinerary literature.[12]

Unlike overland travel, water-borne (especially sea) travel was less easily attempted by the independent traveller under his or her own steam. Affording the time and financial costs of long-distance travel by any means required the individual to be able to command considerable resources whether through personal wealth or coercive power. Moreover, the greater level of financial investment and technical knowledge that was required for almost any kind of riverine or sea-going transport put obstacles in the way of independent travel by these means from the outset. After all, there was no 'do-it-yourself' option in long-distance travel over water as there was over land (i.e. walking). This, even for most well-heeled travellers, meant putting oneself in the hands of another (the ship's master), which necessarily constrained the individual traveller's ability to make or influence decisions about timing, direction, or speed of journey. For the private traveller, finding a passage to the desired destination meant asking around at the port amongst the merchant shipping, and accordingly the timing of departure was not arranged for the convenience of the few fare-paying passengers.[13] In many respects maritime and riverine travel were the

---

[11] Venantius Fortunatus, *Poems* 6.8 and 10.9, relating to two separate trips down the Moselle (and Rhine) in c. AD 566 and 587/8 respectively; on which see J.W. George, *Venantius Fortunatus: A Latin Poet in Merovingian Gaul* (Oxford 1992) 180-185.

[12] R.M. Laurence, *The Roads of Roman Italy: Mobility and Cultural Change* (London 1999) 109. On river craft see L. Casson, *Ships and Seafaring in the Ancient World* (rev. ed. Baltimore 1995) 331-335.

[13] J. Rougé, *Recherches sur l'organisation du commerce maritime en Méditerranée* (École Pratique des Hautes Études - IVe section, Centre de Recherches historiques: Ports-Routes-Trafics 21: Paris 1966) 364; L. Casson, *Travel in*

ancient equivalents of today's scheduled airlines and railways, with land transport playing a similar role to driving by private motor car. Given also that ship's captains are unlikely to have set sail without years of apprenticeship, they will not generally have had to navigate in unfamiliar waters. Hence, *a priori*, in contrast to the demand for details of land routes from the private travelling public, there will have been a smaller market for which information on sea routes might have been collected. This suggests that purely maritime itineraries may always have had a smaller circulation.

There were also a number of technological and environmental conditions that affected the pattern of maritime traffic in particular. These certainly had an impact on the nature and purpose of the ancient maritime itineraries, and that may also have influenced the shape in which they have come down to us. Fernand Braudel emphasised the combined impact of three factors upon the pattern of ship movements in the pre-modern Mediterranean – weather, season, and winds – and these have recently been examined on a scientific basis by Jamie Morton (fig. 8).[14] Navigation by the stars can enable you to keep on course at night and away from land. This allowed large grain ships returning to Alexandria to sail continuously and on a direct course. However, the big limitation was visibility, since clear skies were necessary to see the stars. Winter storms and cloudy skies effectively confined the period of activity of these larger ships to between April and October.[15] The seasonal (etesian) winds that blew steadily from north-northwest to south-southeast during the summer, combined with stronger west to east current in the same season, allowed the grain ships to make the trip with

---

the Ancient World (London 1974) 153-154.

[14] F. Braudel, *The Mediterranean and the Mediterranean World in the Age of Philip II* 2 vols. (London 1972) I, 103-109, 132-135, 246-260; idem, *The Mediterranean in the Ancient World* (London 2001) 15-19, 213-215; J. Morton, *The Role of the Physical Environment in Ancient Greek Seafaring* (Mnemosyne Suppl. 213, Leiden 2001).

[15] For full discussion of the sailing season and night sailing see Casson, *Ships and Seafaring* 270-273; Morton, *Physical Environment* 255-265.

great speed and efficiency.[16] The Elder Pliny relates that it took a new Prefect of Egypt only five days to reach his province from the Straits of Messina, and that a senator starting from Puteoli (Pozzuoli) in Campania arrived in Alexandria in only nine days, despite having only a gentle breeze behind him; by the end of the fourth century, Alexandria had become a regular point of arrival for western pilgrims to the Christian holy sites.[17] The same winds had, in the first century, enabled St. Paul, returning from his second and third missionary tours, to travel directly across open sea from Ephesos (Efes) to Caesarea (Horbat Qesari) in Palestine and from Patara (Yeşilköy) in Lycia to Tyre (Ṣûr).[18] Conversely, the etesian winds meant that the opposite journey was a slow and arduous one, following the indirect route parallel to the coastline either east or west from Alexandria, taking maximum advantage of offshore breezes and tacking back and forth against the wind. This zig-zag course was misinterpreted by at least one aristocratic passenger, alarmed by the prospect of crashing onto rocks, as erratic and deliberately risky behaviour on the part of the captain.[19] The general anticlockwise flow of the current made the easterly route, via the Syrian coast, slightly easier than the western route, and it was onto a ship plying this course from Alexandria to Rome that the prisoner St. Paul was transferred at Myra (Kale) on the Lycian coast.[20] Even so, this route was still fairly slow. In his dialogue *The Ship*, the second-century

[16] On currents and prevailing winds see Morton, *Physical Environment* 37-48 and fig. 1.

[17] Plin., *NH* 19.3-4; E.D. Hunt, *Holy Land Pilgrimage in the Later Roman Empire AD 312-460* (Oxford 1982) 50-82, esp. 72-75.

[18] *Act.Apostol.* 18, 21-22; 21.1-3; Casson, *Travel* 150-152, 158-159.

[19] C.A.J. Skeel, *Travel in the First Century after Christ with Special Reference to Asia Minor* (Cambridge 1901) 84; Casson, *Ships and Seafaring* 270-275. Synesius, *Ep.* 4 (*PG* 66 col. 1329) recounts such a journey westwards from Alexandria to Ptolemais in AD 404; on which see Casson, *Travel* 159-162 and F. Meijer & O.M. van Nijf, *Trade, Transport and Society in the Ancient World: A Sourcebook* (London 1992) 170-176, no. 218.

[20] P. Horden & N. Purcell, *The Corrupting Sea: A Study of Mediterranean History* (Oxford 2000) 137-140; *Acts* 27.6.

writer Lucian describes how, because of storms and adverse winds, it
took one Alexandrian grain ship making the anticlockwise voyage to
Rome seventy days to get only as far as Athens.[21] Thus, without the
assistance of the etesian winds, these great bulk carriers were reduced
to the same methods and speeds of the more mundane coasting or
'tramping' craft that spent much of their time at sea within sight of
land. These ventured into open water only for relatively short and well
tried direct crossings, such as that from Aulon (Vlorë) to the heel of
Italy or from the western tip of Sicily to the north-eastern tip of Africa
Proconsularis. The level of risk associated with open sea crossings
(*traiectus*) can be gauged from the extent of relief expressed by the
series of altars to the goddess Nehalenia at Lugdunum Batauorum
(Leiden), erected in gratitude for the safe conveyance of their cargoes
by merchants engaged in cross-channel shipping.[22]

Keeping close to the shore, steering by landmarks and putting in at
night meant slow but steady progress. This was well suited to the pre-
dominant pattern of ancient merchant shipping, which, as Braudel
emphasised, was not primarily 'destination-conscious' but more like a
travelling bazaar, treating each stop as an opportunity for trading.[23] It
also meant that, weather permitting, this more modest shipping activity
could continue all year round. Accordingly, it was by *orariae naues*
(coasting vessels) that the Younger Pliny was able to reach Bithynia
from Pergamum (Bergama) in September against the prevailing
winds.[24] It is just such a coastal journey, from Rome to Gaul during the

---

[21] Lucian, *Nauigium* 1-6, 9; Skeel, *Travel in the First Century* 82-85.

[22] *AE* 1973, 363-65, 370, 372, 375; *AE* 1975, 646-47, 651; *AE* 1980, 658;
AE 1983, 720-21; Meijer & van Nijf, *Trade, Transport and Society* 87-89, no.
116; on a similar phenomenon associated with the Calabria-Epirus crossing see C. Marangio, "Κέρκυρα nelle linee di rotta di età greca e romana
tra la Grecia e l'Italia" in Laudizi & Marangio (edd.), *Porti, approdi e linee di
rotta* 102-104.

[23] Morton, *Physical Environment* 143-228, esp. 177-206; Braudel, *Mediterranean
in the Age of Philip II* I, 107-108; Horden & Purcell, *The Corrupting Sea* 133-
143.

[24] Plin., *Ep.* 10.15 (*orariis nauibus*), 10.17A.2 (*orarias nauculas*).

winter months of AD 416-417, that Rutilius Namatianus vividly decribes in his poem *De reditu suo* (*On his return*).[25] His account provides important detail as to the practical considerations involved (for example, how every night it is necessary to find a suitable place to put ashore or at least shelter from the open sea). On the first night out (I.239), protection was afforded by the man-made moles of the harbour at Centumcellae (Civitavecchia). The next day the ship anchored in the mouth of the river Umbro (Ombrone) and the crew pitched camp on the sandy beaches of the nearby Pineta del Tombolo:

> We put in at the mouth of the Umbro.
> It is a large river with a safe entrance for
> the tired and frightened sailor who comes there.
> I was more than eager to leave the ship and spend
> at least some time ashore but the sailors
> were anxious and I could only go where they went.
> As we went on, the breeze died with the sun.
> We anchored near the shore and measured out the beach
> for camp. A grove of myrtle gave us wood,
> we pitched our tent on oars that we used for tent poles.
>
> I.338-347 (trans. H. Isbell, p. 230)

An anchorage and beach might serve their purposes but when they did happen upon a convenient town, Namatianus' party took full advantage of its amenities:

> Before noon Falesia came into our sight.
> On that day a fair was in progress and
> the country people had come into town because
> it was the day when Osiris wakes
> and gives new life to the autumn seeds. We sought lodging
> and strolled in a pleasant grove with small ponds.
>
> I.362-67 (trans. H. Isbell, p. 231)

[25] E. Doblhofer, *Rutilius Claudius Namatianus, De Reditu suo siue Iter Gallicum* 2 vols. (Wissenschaftliche Kommentare zu griechischen und lateinischen Schriftstellern, Heidelberg 1972-77); trans. H. Isbell, *The Last Poets of*

Similarly, as Lionel Casson emphasised, the journeys of Cicero from Athens to Ephesos on the way out to his command in Cilicia in 51 BC could have been achieved in three or four days, but actually took two weeks each because the consular governor chose the comfortable option, whereby he was able to rest and recuperate on a different island each night.[26]

In the light of these limitations of season, weather, ancient navigation technology and sailing practice, Braudel characterised the geography of the pre-modern Mediterranean as dominated by desert expanses of open water rarely traversed by mariners. Most maritime activity was restricted to within sight of land, be it mainland or island. Moreover, although admitting a certain level of cross-over, Braudel argued that the two basins of the Mediterranean – east and west of Sicily – formed two separate maritime worlds. Certainly the fast flowing north-south current through the Straits of Messina and the strong west to east current (reinforcing the prevailing wind) in the waters between Sicily and Libya made the crossing of this threshold less than predictable, though the extent to which this 'fault-line' was a hindrance should not be exaggerated.[27] This, then, is the general background against which the maritime itineraries will be examined.

2. The Greek Maritime Itineraries

The tradition of prose descriptions of linear or circular coastal voyages (*periploi*) was well established long before the Roman period in both Punic and Greek literature, the most detailed to survive being that of Pseudo-Scylax of c. 360 BC.[28] As the author c. 105/100 BC of an

---

Imperial Rome (Harmondsworth 1971) 221-241.

[26] Casson, *Travel* 151.

[27] Braudel, *Mediterranean World in the Age of Philip II* I, 103-109, 132-135; cf. Horden & Purcell, *The Corrupting Sea* 133-143.

[28] Dilke, *Greek and Roman Maps* 130-144; Scylax, *Periplus* (Müller, *GGM* I, 15-96).

eleven-book work that was described variously by Marcianus of Heraclea as a *geographia* or *periplus*,[29] and as a resident of the Roman province of Asia, Artemidorus of Ephesos has some claim to be considered in this section. Until recently almost the only remnants of his work were the brief extracts preserved by its occasional quotation in Stephanus Byzantinus' *Ethnica* and, even then, these were quotations via Marcianus' *Epitome* and not from the full text.[30] However, thanks to a recently revealed papyrus find, we now have the first five columns of the full text of book two of Artemidorus' work.[31] This shows it to be more ambitious than simply a description of the coastal regions, even if following the Mediterranean coastline provided the work's organisational principle. While, naturally, recording distances between coastal locations, Artemidorus' primary aim does not appear to have been to provide a guide to the shore. Accordingly, the work of Artemidorus' fellow Asian, Menippus of Pergamum, emerges as the earliest known exemplar from the period of Roman rule of the *periplus* tradition proper.

2.1 Menippus' *Periplus Maris Interni*

Menippus wrote his three-book *Periplus maris interni* (*Circumnavigation of the Inner Sea*) perhaps c. 30 BC, and he certainly had a reputation as a geographical writer by 25 BC, when he is addressed in an epigram by Crinagoras of Mitylene that survives in the Palatine Anthology:[32]

[29] E.g. Marcianus, *Periplus maris exteri* II.19 (Müller, *GGM* I, 551).

[30] Marcianus, *Epitome geographiae Artemidori* (Müller, *GGM* I, 574-576).

[31] C. Gallazzi & B. Kramer, "Artemidor in Zeichensaal. Eine Papyrusrolle mit Text, Landkarte und Skizzenbüchern aus späthellenistischer Zeit", *APF* 44 (1998/9) 190-208; B. & J. Kramer, "Iberia, Hispania und das neue Artemidor-Fragment" in A. Haltenhoff & F.-H. Mutschler (edd.), *Hortus litterarum antiquarum: Festschrift für Hans Armin Gärtner* (Heidelberg 2000) 309-322, esp. 319 ff.

[32] On the date see Müller, *GGM* I, cxxv; A.S.F. Gow & D.L. Page, *The Greek Anthology: The Garland of Philip and Some Contemporary Epigrams* vol. II (Cambridge 1968) 243-244, Crinagoras XXXII.

A voyage to Italy is being prepared for me; to friends
I shall be sent, from whom I have been separated a long time.
I'm searching for a *periplus* that will lead me as a guide
To the islands of the Cyclades, as well as to ancient Scheria.
But, Menippus, as a friend, give me some help; you who have written
A *learned tour* (ἵστορα κύκλον), you who know all geography.

(Palatine Anthology IX 559)

Although the only substantial section to survive covers only part of
the Black Sea coast, it is clear from Marcianus' prefatory summary and
two isolated fragments that Menippus' *Periplus* described the whole of
the Mediterranean littoral as well:

Menippus divided his circumnavigation of the three continents – Asia,
Europe and Libya [Africa] – as follows: the Hellespont, the Propontis [Sea
of Marmara] with the Thracian Bosporus, and the Pontos Euxinos [Black
Sea] on both continents – Asia and Europe – he treated together sepa-
rately, outlining first the Pontos, then the Propontis along with the Hellespont; he began the *periplus* of both continents with the shrine of Zeus
Urios, which lies at the very mouth of Pontos. After this, beginning with
the rest of Europe, he outlines its whole shore up to the Straits of Hercules [Gibraltar] and the Island of Gadeira [Cadiz]. Then crossing to the
opposite land facing the Straits of Hercules, that is to Libya, he outlines it
also and continues it with the description of Asia up to the aforemen-
tioned Hellespont.   (Marcianus, *Epitome* 6)

Although Menippus' base, Pergamum (Bergama), is not itself
directly on the coast, the work's organisation nevertheless clearly
reflects a Pergamene focus; since, while the mouths of the Bosporus
and Hellespont are natural topographical thresholds, their relative
proximity to Pergamum surely recommended them to Menippus as the
termini of his *periplus*. Indeed the remains of the list of contents reveals
that after describing the coast from Aiga/Kane (Bademlı) to Adramyttium (Edremit) – that is, where the *periplus* passes closest to Pergamum
– the coastal itinerary is interrupted by a section entitled 'the distances
between cities by land', before resuming the treatment of the coast
from Adramyttium on to the terminal point at Sigeum (Kumkale) at

the mouth of the Hellespont.[33] This interloping terrestrial section no doubt listed distances from Pergamum to the towns just described along the coast, so anchoring the *periplus* to local geography for a Pergamum-based readership.

It is worthy of note that the anticlockwise direction of Menippus' description of the coastline of both the Black Sea and Mediterranean corresponds closely with the prevailing direction of the surface currents along those coasts during the sailing season.[34] Internally the three major parts of the *Periplus* were divided into subsections defined by summaries of the total distances between the more important locations. Within these the coastal itinerary is described by a series of measurements from one stage to the next in the form *from X to Y, stades Z.* The general style of the work can be gauged from the first subsection of the Black Sea portion, which traces the coastline in an anticlockwise direction from the shrine of Zeus Urios on the Bosporus (Anadolu Kavağı) to Heraclea Pontica (Ereğli):

From the shrine of Zeus Urios to the river Rheba are 90 stades. From the Rheba to the Black Point it is 150 stades. From Black Point to the river and village of Artane it is 150 stades. Artane also has a little harbour for small boats and nearby lies a small island that shelters the harbour. From the river Artane to the river and village of Psillios it is 140 stades. From the river Psillios to the river <and village of> Calpa it is 210 stades. This is a trading-post (*emporion*) of the people of Heraclea and the river has a good harbour. From the river Calpa to the island of Thynias it is 60 stades. From the island of Thynias to the navigable river Sangarios [Sakarya] it is 200 stades. From the river Sangarios to the river Hypios it is 180 stades. From the river Hypios to the city of Dias it is 60 stades. Dias has an anchorage for ships. From the city of Dias to the river and trading-post of Elaios it is 90 stades. From the river Elaios to the river and trading-post of Cales it is 120 stades. From the river Cales to the great city of Heraclea it is 80 stades. From this Heraclea to the city of Apollonia [Sozopol] that is in Europe, situated with its back to the county of the Thracians, it is

---

[33] Marcianus, *Epitome* (Müller, *GGM* I, 565).
[34] Morton, *Physical Environment* 37-39; see our fig. 8.

<2>000 stades. The total from the shrine of Zeus Urios to the city of Heraclea is 1530. Sailing by the direct route from the shrine to the city of Heraclea it is 1200.

So Menippus gives a detailed, but impersonal, account of the features of the coast, unadorned with historical or mythological details. Beyond the bare listing of distances, he restricts comment to features pertinent to a ship-owner or ship's captain, such as the presence and quality of harbours and anchorages, as well as *emporia*, and elsewhere the direction of prevailing winds. In contrast, for instance, on mentioning Heraclea in his *Periplus*, Arrian could not refrain from adding that historically its dialect was Dorian and that it was a Megarian foundation.[35] While interesting to modern scholars, these hardly qualify as pieces of information crucial for the contemporary traveller.

However, might this contrast with Arrian be a false one? For, from Crinagoras' verse we might expect Menippus' work to have originally included a slightly fuller treatment, including cultural material. After all, in employing the Homeric term 'Scheria' for Corcyra (Corfù), Crinagoras would seem to be suggesting that the desired work would include historical and mythological information. Such content would indeed fit more comfortably with Crinagoras' allusion to the work as 'learned'. Moreover, given Crinagoras' social position and role (not as ship's captain, but as Mytilenean envoy to Rome and writer of epigrams), when he says that he needs Menippus' work, does he really need it as a practical guide to navigation or as something more akin to a Michelin *Guide Vert*, from which he might derive edifying information on the various places he passes? If the epigram does refer to the *periplus* we have, one might wonder whether our current text represents an abbreviation of the original that has deliberately omitted the cultural and historical material. To decide, it is necessary to consider the history of the text in some detail.

Of the three extant manuscripts containing Menippus, two are sixteenth-century derivatives of the earliest surviving: Paris, Bibliothèque

---

[35] Arrian, *Periplus* 13.3.

Nationale, codex graecus suppl. 443 of the late thirteenth century. In this, the text of Menippus occupies the pages numbered 49-60 but it has suffered in two ways. Firstly, the opening is missing because between pages 48 and 49 this codex has lost its original sixth quire, so that Menippus' text begins abruptly with the last few lines of the list of contents (p. 49, lines 1-3); secondly, the continuous text breaks off suddenly at the village of Chadisios just after Amisos (Samsun), followed by a scribal note to indicate that the rest is missing (λείπη), a blank page (p. 61), and a note at the top of page 62 indicating that another work has begun. All of which indicates that the archetype from which this manuscript was copied was already defective at this point. Without head or tail, the work was for a long time generally misidentified as an epitome of Artemidorus' *Periplus*, until the correct attribution was restored in Carl Müller's edition of 1854.[36] However, Müller retained its characterisation as an epitome. Nevertheless, Aubrey Diller pointed out that Marcianus in his preface draws a distinction in terminology between his previous *epitome* of Artemidorus, his own *periplus* of the Outer Sea, and his *ekdosis* (i.e. edition) of Menippus. This editing, Diller argues, consisted in the provision of the preface, of some minor updating of toponymy, and the addition of subheadings to break up Menippus' text into provincial subsections.[37] On balance, it is probable that Marcianus preserved Menippus' text largely unaltered. Such brevity in Menippus' original would certainly accord with the likely difference in scale of extent between his own work and that of Artemidorus. Even given the imprecision of the 'book' as a measure of length, it is striking that Artemidorus' work ran to eleven books, whereas Marcianus tells us that Menippus' comprised only three: I. The Black Sea; II. The Hellespont to Cadiz; III. Straits of Gibraltar to the mouth of the Hellespont.[38] This is most plausibly attributed to the fact that Artemidorus described the political and historical geography of

---

[36] Müller, *GGM* I, 563-573.

[37] Diller, *Minor Greek Geographers* 147-149, analysing Marcianus' own description of his editorial contribution (Müller, *GGM* I, 567).

[38] Marcianus, *Epitome* 3 (Müller, *GGM* I, 566).

those countries bordering the Mediterranean and Black Sea, while Menippus confined himself throughout to a detailed description of the coastline alone. That the indications of distance were the dominant feature is further suggested by the emperor Constantine Porphyrogenitus' citation of Menippus in his *De thematibus* as 'he who had written out the stade-measurements (σταδιασμοί) of the whole *oecumene*'.[39] In this context, it seems unlikely that Menippus' *Periplus* would have fulfilled Crinagoras' needs. Rather than expressing the desire for a copy of this work, the epigram is more easily understood as asking Menippus to compose a new work that would perform the function of cultural guide. If the 'learned tour' does allude to the surviving *periplus*, then we might take Crinagoras' 'learned' in the sense of 'empirically researched'.[40]

2.2 The *Stadiasmus Maris Magni*

The real nature of Menippus' work thus discerned, its distinction from the periegetic and geographical literature, on the one hand, and its close affinity to the anonymous *Stadiasmus maris magni*, on the other, are made more apparent. The close similarity in structure between the *Stadiasmus* and Menippus was noted by Diller, although he did not consider the *Stadiasmus* in detail because it fell outside the Marcianic corpus of geographers with which he was chiefly concerned. Indeed until recently the *Stadiasmus* has suffered relative neglect at the hands of modern scholars generally interested in works of a more geographical nature.[41] The only comprehensive commentary remains that by Carl

---

[39] Const. Porphyr., *De them.* I.2 [18, 5-7 ed. Bonn]; on which see Diller, *Minor Greek Geographers* 42.

[40] See the commentary of Gow & Page, *Greek Anthology* II, 243-244, Crinagoras XXXII.

[41] It did not rate a mention in R. Güngerich, *Die Küstenbeschreibung in der griechischen Literatur* (Orbis Antiquus 4, Münster 1950); since superseded by G. Hartinger, *Die Periplusliteratur* (diss. Salzburg 1992) (non vidi). Even P. Janni, *La mappa e il periplo*, cites it only once (p. 116 n.94), in relation to the

Müller accompanying his edition and parallel Latin text in *Geographi Graeci Minores* vol. I of 1855 and, to my knowledge, there is as yet no translation into any modern language.[42] In fact our knowledge of the *Stadiasmus maris magni* or *Matritensis*, as it is sometimes known, depends on its preservation in a single tenth-century Byzantine manuscript now in Madrid, where it is found incorporated into the *Chronicle of Hippolytus* (of AD 234/5).[43] As a result, the most recent critical edition of the *Stadiasmus* is in fact contained in Adolf Bauer's edition of the *Chronicle* in the *GCS* series of Hippolytus' works; this incorporates the comments of Otto Cuntz on the *Stadiasmus* in the "Vorarbeit" to the *GCS* edition.[44] Although generally dated later than the first century AD, the only firm *terminus post quem* is provided by the reference to 'Caesarea' in Palestine (*Stad.* 272 [527]), which only received this name from King Herod between 22 and 10/9 BC.[45] Unfortunately, its inclusion in the manuscript of Hippolytus' *Chronicle* does not provide a *terminus ante quem*. For, neither appearing in the surviving contents page of the *Chronicle* nor having left any trace in those works derived from it, the *Stadiasmus* clearly did not form part of the original full text of the *Chronicle*, but was rather interpolated into it some time later to fill out

concept of an island 'looking to the east' (*Stad.* 336 [594]). Cf. now Uggeri in Laudizi & Marangio (edd.), *Porti, approdi e linee di rotta* 33-46 for an extended analysis.

[42] Müller, *GGM* I, 427-514; text reproduced in Y. Kamal, *Monumenta Cartographica Africae et Aegypti* 5 vols (Leiden 1926-1951), as part of vol. 2.1: *Ptolemée et époque greco-romaine*. A monograph is promised by J.W. Ermatinger of Southeast Missouri State University.

[43] Madrid, Biblioteca Nacional, codex graecus 4701 (previously 121).

[44] A. Bauer, *Hippolytus Werke* IV: *Die Chronik* (GCS 36, Berlin 1929), revised ed. R. Helm (GCS 46, Berlin 1955); O. Cuntz, "Der Stadiasmus Maris Magni" in A. Bauer, *Die Chronik des Hippolytos im Matritensis graecus 121* (Texte und Untersuchungen zur Geschichten der altchristlichen Literatur 29 [n.F. 14], 1, Leipzig 1905) ch. 5, 243-276. Reference to the *Stadiasmus* is here made by the section numbers of Müller's *GGM* edition with those of the continuous text of Hippolytus' *Chronicle* in brackets.

[45] Müller, *GGM* I, cxxvii-viii and Cuntz in Bauer, *Chronik des Hippolytos* 245.

its geographical section.[46] The occasionally barbarous grammar led some to favour a date as late as the fifth century AD, but the frequent noting of pagan shrines and the complete absence of Christian references renders this unlikely.[47] Until epigraphic evidence demonstrated the existence of harbour installations at the mouth of the Wadi Lebdah by AD 61/62, the description of the city of Lepcis Magna as without a harbour (*Stad.* 93 [339]) was thought to provide a *terminus ante quem* of c. AD 200, when Septimius Severus endowed his home town with a new harbour.[48] Most recently, on the basis of the *Stadiasmus'* distortion of the name of the island of Caudos/Gaudos on the south side of Crete into 'Claudia' (*Stad.* 328 [586]), Giovanni Uggeri has argued that the chronological window should be narrowed to specifically the AD 50s and 60s (i.e. because of the influence of the imperial titulature of Claudius and Nero).[49] However, there is no reason to suppose that this banal error, shared with the texts of several other authors, need originally have stood in the text of the *Stadiasmus*

---

[46] Cuntz in Bauer, *Chronik des Hippolytos* 243; Bauer/Helm, *Chronik* 2-18 (had the *Stadiasmus* formed an integral part of the *Chronicle*, it ought to have appeared between nos. 5 and 6 of the contents list).

[47] G. Charles-Picard, *La civilization de l'Afrique romaine* (Paris 1959) 377 n.85; K. Vogel, "Byzantine Science" in J.M. Hussey (ed.), *The Cambridge Medieval History* vol. 4 (Cambridge 1967) 295. Cf. Cuntz in Bauer, *Chronik des Hippolytos* 249-50, 253.

[48] Müller, *GGM* I, cxxvii-viii, with 461-62 note; Cuntz in Bauer, *Chronik des Hippolytos* 244; Rougé, *Organisation du commerce maritime* 133 n.4. Cf. J.M. Reynolds & J.B. Ward-Perkins, *The Inscriptions of Roman Tripolitania* (London 1952) 341; A. Di Vita, "Un passo dello Σταδιασμός τῆς Μεγάλης Θαλάσσης ed il porto ellenistico di Leptis Magna" in J.-P. Boucher et al. (edd.), *Mélanges de philosophie, de littérature et d'histoire ancienne offerts à Pierre Boyancé* (Collection EFR 22, Rome 1974) 229-49.

[49] G. Uggeri, "Stadiasmus Maris Magni: un contributo per la datazione" in M. Khanoussi, P. Ruggeri, C. Vismara (edd.), *L'Africa romana XI: Atti del XI Convegno di studio, Cartagine, 15-18 dicembre 1994* (Pubb. del Dip. di Storia dell'Univ. degli Studi di Sassari 28, Oziero 1996) 277-85; idem in Laudizi & Marangio (edd.), *Porti, approdi e linee di rotta* 43-46.

rather than stemmed from a subsequent copyist; nor is this the only placename that has suffered from scribal corruption of this type.[50] Moreover, that the Cilician town of Elaeussa is still so called (*Stad.* 172-73 [424-25]), rather than Sebaste, suggests that the data for this section at least derives from before the end of the Augustan period. Thus, whether as a compilation of disparate records or the empirical observations of a single author, there is, in fact, nothing to preclude the *Stadiasmos* from belonging to within a few decades of Menippus' *Periplus*, as Diller suggested.[51]

The original coverage of the *Stadiasmus* was certainly comparable to Menippus' work, though it probably did not include the Black Sea along with the Mediterranean. However, as with Menippus, the *Stadiasmus* survives only in a mutilated and truncated form. The introduction to the work, which describes it as a *stadiasmus* or *periplus* of the 'Great Sea' (i.e. the Mediterranean), implies that the entire coast of the Mediterranean will be covered. However, as it stands in the manuscript, the description that immediately follows claims rather that the *periplus* will be explained 'beginning from the Pharos island at Alexandria to Dioscuris on the Black Sea, and then of the European shore from the shrine that lies opposite the shrine of the Chalcedonians to the Pillars of Hercules and Gadeira [Cadiz]' (*Stad.* pr. [240]). This would suggest that it took the reader from Alexandria by way of the Asian shore, through the Bosporus and then round eastwards along the Black Sea coast to Dioscuri(a)s/Sebastopolis in the Caucasus,[52] followed by a big jump back to the Thracian Bosporus as the starting point of the description of the European shore round to the Straits of Gibraltar – a somewhat more partial and bitty coverage than the title 'of the Great Sea' implies. While Dioscurias has some plausibility as a terminus, as

---

[50] 'Claudos/Claude': *Act.Apostol.* 27, 16, Ptolemy, *Geog.* 3.15.8, p. 245, Hierocles, *Synecdem.* p. 651, 2; cf. the familiar name of the island 'Samos' for the less familiar town of Amos on the Carian coast (*Stad.* 267-68 [522-23]).

[51] Diller, *Minor Greek Geographers* 49-50.

[52] Dioscuris (Ps.-Scylax 81), Dioscurias (Arrian, *Periplus* 17.1, 2; 18.1).

the extreme outpost of empire when Arrian visited it as governor,[53] such a structure would leave the Black Sea untidily incomplete and the African shore from the Straits to Alexandria completely neglected. And, indeed, it is contradicted by the opening portion of the *periplus* itself, which begins by tracing the African shore westwards from Alexandria. Thus Müller was surely right in discerning that the introduction has suffered from two instances of relatively banal scribal error: first, an instance of haplography (*saute de même au même*) over two occurrences of 'Pharitis' and, second, corruption of the shrine 'of Zeus Urios' into 'Dioscuris'.[54] Accordingly the description ought to read:

> ... I have decided to explain the *stadiasmus* or *periplus* of the Great Sea to you in the most precise detail, so that you will become learned in these things by reading it, beginning from the island of Pharos at Alexandria <with the Libyan shore as far as the Pillars of Hercules, then that of Asia, starting once again from the island of Pharos at Alexandria,> as far as the shrine of Zeus Urios that lies on the Pontos, and then that of Europe from the shrine that lies opposite that of the Chalcedonians up to the Pillars of Hercules and Gadeira, wishing to be helpful to all men.

Under this reconstruction, therefore, the *Stadiasmus*, unlike Menippus, omitted the Black Sea and instead restricted itself to the Mediterranean proper, which it described not by a complete tour but into two symmetrical journeys beginning from Alexandria and ending at the Straits of Gibraltar: the first clockwise, the second anticlockwise, omitting the Black Sea by interrupting at the shrine of the Chalcedonians, i.e. of Zeus Urios (Anadolu Kavağı), and resuming at the opposite shrine of the Byzantines (Rumeli Kavağı). Of this original extent the following survives:

1-127 (242-376): description of the North African shore from Alexandria westwards to Utica. This then jumps mid-sentence to Carnae on the Phoenician coast between Aradus (Ṭarṭūs) and Balaneae (Bâniyâs) because

---

[53] Arrian, *Periplus* 17-18.
[54] Müller, *GGM* I, 428 note.

of the loss of a folio already in the archetype, which has gone unnoticed or been patched by the scribe, rather than because of a defect in the Madrid manuscript at this point. This lacuna would have contained the remaining description of the North African coast from Utica to the Pillars of Hercules and the first part of the route from Alexandria anticlockwise up the coast of Palestine.[55]

128-271 (377-526): from Carnae northwards up the Syrian coast and then westwards along Cilician, Pamphylian, Lycian, and Carian coasts as far as the island of Rhodes.

271-272 (526-527): list of distances point-to-point from Rhodes to various places, including the shrine of the Byzantines (271) and direct to Alexandria (272).

273 (528): Rhodes via Cyclades to the Scyllaeum point in the Argolid in the Peloponnese.

274-279 (529-534): list of distances point-to-point between Cos and Myndos (Gümüşlük) and various locations in Caria, the Dodecanese, and Cyclades.

280 (535): Cos to Delos via the islands of Calymnos, Leros, Patmos, and Myconos.

281 (536): Myndos to Attica via the channel between Calymnos and Leros, Lebinthos, Amorgos, Donusa, Naxos, and Cythnos.

282 (537): Cos to Delos via the islands of Leros, Lebinthos, Cinaros, and Amorgos.

283 (538): Cos to Carystus on Euboea and the nearby Petalian islands via the islands of Leros, Patmos, Delos, Syros, and Andros.

284 (539): list of distances point-to-point from Delos to other islands of the Cyclades.

285-296 (540-552): resumption of coastal itinerary from Myndos to Miletus and Samos.

297-317 (553-575): circumnavigation of Cyprus clockwise and then distances direct from various points on the island to Anemurium (Anamur) in Cilicia, Pelusium (Al Farama) in Egypt, and Ascalon (Ashqelon) in Palestine.

318-355 (576-613): circumnavigation of Crete clockwise from Point Samonium (Sideros; 'Salmone' in *Act.Apostol.* 27, 7) at its north-easterly extremity.

---

[55] Müller, *GGM* I, 472 note; Bauer/Helm, *Chronik* p. 53, 19-22.

The starting point at the Pharos and omission of the Black Sea reflect a strongly Alexandrian viewpoint, so that it seems most likely that its anonymous author was working in Alexandria which, as the rival Hellenistic cultural centre to Pergamum, is very appropriate as the location of this counterpart to Menippus. Since none of their surviving portions overlap, it is impossible to judge to what extent the *Stadiasmus* might represent a reworking of Menippus' material. There are clearly similarities in structure. Both employ the *from X to Y, stades Z* formula and subdivide the coastal itinerary into sections summed up by subtotals of the distances, but this could derive from nothing more than their shared purpose, the practical nature of which the author of the *Stadiasmus* emphasises at the end of the introduction (continuing on immediately from that section quoted above):

> I shall make clear the intervals of distance that separate Europe from Asia and I shall also describe the distances from one island to another, how many islands there are, how they should appear to those sailing past, the kinds of wind there are, which winds one can make use of, and shall show you what sailing is in reality.

The direct address to the reader at the end is indicative of a major difference of style between Menippus and the *Stadiasmus*. Where the former was relentlessly impersonal, the latter personalises the account by addressing the reader as a potential navigator with sporadic use of the personal pronoun 'you' and second-person verbs. Another difference is that, whereas Menippus' description is expressed in full sentences, the *Stadiasmus* uses a brief note form. Moreover, although not immediately apparent from the modern editions, in the sole manuscript, after the introduction and a heading 'Stadiasmus of the Sea', the main body of the text is laid out in two columns. Each stage has its own entry and to the right in a separate column appear the distance figures preceded by the abbreviation στάδ., with the variant στάδδ. indicating the summary totals.[56] There seems no reason to doubt that

---

[56] Cuntz in Bauer, *Chronik des Hippolytos* 255, with plate IV, illustrating cod. Matr. gr. 4701, fol. 63 verso.

this layout is derived from the archetype and is, of course, the same practical layout found in the Latin itinerary literature. The following translation of the very first section (1-19 [242-261]) aims to transmit the flavour of the original (the distance figures are given as in the manuscript with Müller's suggested emendations in brackets):

1	From Alexandria to Chersonesos; there is a harbour.	stad. 2
2	From Chersonesos to Dysmai; there is a harbour for no more than a thousand measures/weight.	<stad.> 70
3	From Dysmai to Plinthine; there are sea swells; the place is harbourless.	stad. 90
4	From Plinthine to Taposiris; the city is harbourless; a shrine of Osiris.	stad. 70 [90]
5	From Taposiris to Chio; there is a village; low rocks visible.	stad. 70 [90]
6	From Chio to Glaucos.	stad. 80
7	From Glaucos to Antiphrai; the place is choppy.	stad. 80
8	From Antiphrai to Derra; there is a bay and in summertime water is to be had.	stad. 70 [90]
9	From Derra to Zephyron; there is a harbour and they have sea swells.	stad. 400 [170]
10	From Zephyron to Pezone; some stades from here is a reef and it is called Myrmex; and the promontory is called Rocky.	stad. 110
11	From Pezone to Pnigeus; the promontory is low-lying; going right takes you into rocky shallows.	stad. 70 [90]
12	From Pnigeus to Phoinicus; there are twin little islands; a bay behind them, deep enough for heavy vessels; there is rockpool water in the gorge.	stad. 140
13	From Phoinicus to Hermaia; anchor, keeping the promontory to your right; there is water to be had in the tower.	stad. 70 [90]

14   From Hermaia to Leuce Acte [White Shore]; a small   stad. 20
      low island lies nearby, at a distance of 2 stades from
      the mainland; it is a shelter for heavy vessels during
      westerly winds; on the mainland, under the head-
      land, is an extensive bay for all sorts of boats; a
      shrine of Apollo with a famous oracle; and water is
      to be had near the shrine.

15   From Leuce Acte to Zygris; there is a small island   stad. 70 [90]
      there; anchor with it to your left; there is water to be
      had in the sand.

16   From Zygris to Ladamantia; a reasonably large   stad. 20
      island lies nearby; anchor with it to your right; the
      harbour is for every type of wind; it has water.

17   From Ladamantia to Calamaion; there is a   stad. 40
      promontory, having a reef to the right of the bay.

18   From Calamaion to Graias Gony [Old Woman's   stad. 70
      Knee]; the promontory is rocky, having a reef in the
      shallows; there is a tree on the shore; there is a bay
      and water to be had under the tree; watch out for
      the southerly wind.

19   From Graias Gony to Arton; the headland is rocky,   stad. 120
      does not have a bay and the headland has two horns
      that protrude out into the sea almost like islands; on
      rounding it, you see the city of Paraitonion.

      The total of all from Alexandria to Paraitonion
      comes to: stadd. 1550

This is certainly no cultural and historical *periegesis*. The general character is similar to Menippus, albeit with slightly different emphases and perhaps slightly more circumstantial detail. Absent are the mentions of *emporia* and instead there is a consistent concern to locate sources of fresh water. Both differences can be ascribed to the different nature of the terrain here, which is a sparsely inhabited, inhospitable, desert environment. It is argued that the anonymous author uses topographical vocabulary such as the variations of *hormos* (natural bay) – *hyphormos* and *panormos* – in a consistent and precisely technical fashion.[57] However, this level of detail is not maintained in the other surviving, Asiatic, portion. This may suggest that the north African portion was uniquely enriched by the addition of empirical detail, perhaps reflecting the personal knowledge of the author/compiler. Combined with the often less than perfect grammar, the *Stadiasmus* as a whole gives the impression of a functional product, without any literary pretensions, intended for practical use by its readership. However, given the general absence of compass directions, it could not be used without the experience of a pilot.[58] Nevertheless, the unadorned style and concentration on practical detail common to both Menippus and the *Stadiasmus* mark them out from much of the rest of the *periplus* and periegetic literature as true counterparts to the more familiar Latin, and predominantly terrestrial, itinerary literature of the Roman period.

3. Rivers and Maritime Routes in the Latin Itineraries

The Roman *itineraria* (route-guides) that have been preserved through the medieval manuscript tradition have tended to be exploited as a quarry for information on the Roman road network. In the category of *itineraria* I include not only the itinerary collection known as the *Itinerarium Antonini*, and the *Itinerarium Burdigalense* (which

---

[57] Rougé, *Organisation du commerce maritime* 111-117; J.H. Little, "Harbours and settlements in Cyrenaica", *Society for Libyan Studies, Annual Report* 9 (1977/78), 43-45.

[58] There are two references to navigation by the constellations – in relation to Aries – (*Stad.* 272 [527], 280 [535]), both relating to open water crossings between islands, though there is frequent relative orientation – e.g., left, right – in the routes through the Aegean islands (*Stad.* 273-281 [528-536]). Striking is the general absence of reference to wind directions, despite the survival of several wind roses (i.e. wind diagrams) from antiquity; cf. Uggeri in Laudizi & Marangio (edd.), *Porti, approdi e linee di rotta* 72-75.

recounts a set of journeys between Bordeaux and Jerusalem in AD
333),[59] but also the *Tabula Peutingeriana,* whose network of red lines it
is all too tempting to imagine as a diagram of the public road system.
As a result of this focus on translating lists of stations into physical
roads, the status of the *itineraria* as recording routes that might make
use of both land and water along their length has sometimes been
overlooked.

3.1 The *Itinerarium Antonini*

Compared to the narrow thread by which the transmission of
Menippus and the *Stadiasmus* hangs, the *Itinerarium Antonini* (*Route-
Guide of Antoninus*) is attested in one form or another in over twenty
manuscripts, six of them of twelfth-century date or earlier, and forming a two-branched tradition.[60] Like Menippus and the *Stadiasmus,* it
appears to be a private initiative rather than a government-organised
collation of central files.[61] The original practical utility of the land
itineraries to the private traveller is not in doubt, although they have
been preserved in the manuscript tradition perhaps because collected
together by a compiler with primarily geographical interests.[62] For, as
it is, the *Itinerarium Antonini* is composed of a number of sub-collec-
tions of quite disparate material, amongst which is some material that
cannot be any earlier than the Diocletianic period. Concentrating on
the terrestrial sections, Pascal Arnaud has proposed a date no earlier
than AD 338 for the collection as a whole, though Giovanni Uggeri

---

[59]   The latest critical edition of the *It.Burd.* is that of F. Glorie, *Itineraria et alia
geographica* (Corpus Christianorum, Series Latina 175, Turnhout 1965) 1-26.
[60]   Cuntz, *Itineraria Romana* I, iv-v.
[61]   R.W.B. Salway, "Travel, *Itineraria* and *Tabellaria*" in C.E.P. Adams & R.M.
Laurence (edd.), *Travel and Geography in the Roman World* (London 2001) 36-
47; C.R. Whittaker, "Mental maps: seeing like a Roman" in P. McKechnie
(ed.), *Thinking Like a Lawyer: Essays on Legal History and General History for
John Crook on his Eightieth Birthday* (Leiden 2002) 93-95, 109-110.
[62]   Salway in Adams & Laurence (edd.), *Travel and Geography* 39-43.

has recently suggested a date as late as the fifth or sixth century for one component of the maritime section.[63] The collection was organised by its compiler into two complementary sections, entitled *itinerarium prouinciarum* (*route-guide of the provinces*) and *itinerarium maritimum* (*maritime route-guide*), both of which take their starting point beyond the Pillars of Hercules. This is obviously a convenient geographical entry point but it may, nevertheless, reflect the origin of the compiler, as was the case with Menippus and probably also the anonymous author of the *Stadiasmus*. The compiler of the itinerary may, therefore, have been working in Spain or Mauretania. The provenance of the earliest extant manuscript may be relevant in this respect; it was written in an early seventh-century Visigothic uncial hand and is now housed in the library of the Escorial outside Madrid.[64] This manuscript also, uniquely, opens with a vignette of the Pillars of Hercules, labelled in the middle 'Fretum Gaditanum', to the left 'Mauritania', the right 'Hispania', and underneath 'Africa'. This would seem to reflect a special pride in the location, either by author or scribe.

3.1.a) Rivers and travel by water in the *itinerarium prouinciarum*

Although the *Itinerarium Antonini* is organised into two complementary sections, entitled *itinerarium prouinciarum* and *itinerarium maritimum* respectively, their contents do not constitute a simple binary opposition of 'terrestrial' as opposed to 'maritime' itineraries. For neither entirely comprises land or sea *itinera* (routes).[65] Right from the outset

---

[63] P. Arnaud, "L'itineraire d'Antonin: un témoin de la literature du Bas-Empire", *Geographia Antica* 2 (1993) 33-49; Uggeri in Laudizi & Marangio (edd.), *Porti, approdi e linee di rotta* 53-59.

[64] Biblioteca del Escorial, ms. R II 18; E.A. Lowe, *Codices Latini Antiquiores* vol. IX (Oxford 1966) 1631.

[65] As observed by S. Crogiez, "Le *cursus publicus* et la circulation des informations officielles par mer" in J. Andreau & C. Virlouvet (edd.), *L'information et la mer dans le monde antique* (Collection EFR 297, Rome 2002) 57.

it is plain that the *itinera* of the *itinerarium prouinciarum* do not simply describe travel by road, because the second section of the very first *iter* (from the outpost Mercurii on the south-western fringe of Mauretania to Carthage) prescribes that 'from Tingis one sails by the coast up to Portus Diuini' (*a Tingi litoribus nauigatur usque ad Portus Diuinos*: 9, 1-31, 7). The verb used (*nauigare*) leaves no doubt that a boat trip rather than simply a coastal road is envisaged, even though the distances are measured in miles (*milia passuum*) not stades. The choice of sea over land here is dictated by the rugged and barren nature of the Mediterranean shore of Mauretania Tingitana. A similar switch from land to water is advised in the route from Rome to Aquileia, though for different reasons. Here, because of the marshy ground and presence of (partly-manmade) navigable waterways, one is advised to sail the 'Seven Seas' (i.e. the lagoons around the mouth of the Po) for the section from Ravenna to Altinum: *ab Arimino recto itinere Rauenna m.p. XXXIII, inde nauigatur Septem Maria Altinum usque, inde Concordia m.p. XXXI* (126, 5-9).[66]

Elsewhere a switch to travel by boats coasting or 'tramping' along the coastline would seem to be signalled by the heading *per loca maritima*. Despite the absence of any verb specifically to indicate sailing, the change from miles to stades as the measure for distance leaves little room for doubt in the route listed from Bracara (Braga) northwards to Brigantium (A Coruña). The sequence of distances in *milia passuum* is broken by three given in *stadia*, indicating that the traveller is expected to take to the water for this stretch in the region of Vicus Spacorum (Vigo), where the fjord-like topography makes this by far the most direct route (423, 6-424, 7):

Item per loca maritima a Bracara Asturicam usque:

---

[66] On the system of navigable *fossae* linking Ravenna with the various mouths of the Po and the Venetian lagoons, see R. Uggeri, "Vie di terra e via d'acqua tra Aquileia e Ravenna in età romana" in *Aquileia e Ravenna* (Antichità Altoadriatiche 13, Udine 1978) 45-79; Laurence, *Roads of Roman Italy* 115-120.

Aquis Celenis	m.p. CLXV
Vico Spacorum	stadia CXCV
Ad Duos Pontes	stadia CL
Glandimiro	stadia CLXXX
Atricondo	m.p. XXII
Brigantium	m.p. XXX

However, where the phrase *per loca maritima* occurs with a route given entirely in miles there is room for ambiguity as to whether sea travel is intended or not. Such an example comes in the section on Sicily: *a Lilybaeo per maritima loca Tyndaridem usque* (90, 6-7; cf. 97, 7: *ab Hyccaris maritima*). Without the use of stades, the phrase might be taken to refer simply to a road along the coast, as opposed to further inland. However, when the same phrase is used in relation to the route from Agrigentum to Syracuse, the employment of sea-borne craft is certified by the qualification of various of the stops as either *refugium* (shelter) or *plag<i>a* (beach), i.e. indications of their usefulness as places to land or keep a boat safe from rough seas. Even if these qualifications are later glosses to the original text,[67] their presence demonstrates nevertheless that this section had been used as a guide by at least one water-borne traveller. Thus there can be little doubt that, on one occasion at least, *per maritima loca* was taken to mean 'by the sea route'. However, as in the example from Bracara to Brigantium above, the presence of the phrase prefacing a list of stations cannot always be taken to mean that all the constituent stages are to be made by water. For, in the route *per loca maritima* described from Epirus to Thessaly via Athens, it is simply implausible that all the stages (e.g. Delphi) could be achieved by water (324, 1-328, 6); rather it must have involved switching to and fro between land and sea. An example of the natural mixing of road and sea transport in this way is provided by the third *Satire* of Lucilius Iunior, which recounts the poet's journey from Rome to Sicily. In this he describes

---

[67] As suspected by the editor of the Teubner edition, Otto Cuntz (*Itineraria Romana* I, p. 14).

how he considers the distances with care and weighs up his options, before deciding to take the road (the via Appia) to Campania but on reaching Puteoli to switch to travelling by sea. From Puteoli he 'tramps' along the coast past Salernum (Salerno) and Paestum as far as Cape Palinurus (Palinuro) in Lucania, at which point the boat changes course and heads across open sea towards the Straits of Messina via the Aeolian islands.[68]

Obviously, even if Lucilius had taken the land route, it would have involved him in crossing water at the Straits of Messina. Numerous river crossings would be a mundane part of any long-distance journey by road. The styles of the itineraries making up the *Itinerarium Antonini* vary quite considerably, but most are bare lists of toponyms that do not differentiate between a settlement and a landmark (though the latter obviously might frequently lend its name to the former). Occasionally rivers are explicitly labelled as *fluuius* or *flumen*, as, for instance, in the isolated examples of the river Frigidus in the Julian Alps (128, 7) and of the Var on the route following the Via Augusta between Nice and Antibes (297, 1: *Varum flumen*). The route listed from Mediolanum (Milan) to the toe of Italy (98, 2-106, 4) is unusually informative in this respect. It indicates the presence of a river on no less than four occasions, three times with the formula 'ad fluuium X' and once uniquely with *super*, i.e. 'over', 'above', or 'beyond' (103, 1: *super* [*Tha*]*mari* (sic) *fluuium*).[69] More frequently a river is cited simply as a landmark with the standard formula 'ad X', indicating the distance 'to' or 'at' that point. Such is the case with two consecutive stations on the route from Rome to the Straits of Messina: *ad Tana<g>rum m.p. XXVIII, ad Calorem m.p. XXIIII*. Where a bridge had given rise to a significant

---

[68] Lucilius frags. 71-117 in E. Baehrens, *Fragmenta Poetarum Romanarum* (Leipzig 1886) 150-155; J.-M. André & M.-F. Baslez, *Voyager dans l'Antiquité* (Paris 1993) 95-97.

[69] *Ad fluuium Bradanum* (104, 3), *ad fluuium Sabutum* (105, 5), *ad fluuium Angitulam* (106, 1). Similarly: *ad Sabutum fluuium* (110, 8) and *ad Atrum flumen* (418, 2), on the route from Ebora (Evora) to Augusta Emerita (Merida).

settlement, the toponym alerted the traveller to the junction of road and river (e.g. *Pons Tiluri*, i.e. Trilj in Dalmatia: 337, 5). Elsewhere, even though the watercourse remained anonymous, the simple indication of a bridge served to warn of the occurrence of a river crossing, whether noted as a landmark (*ad pontem*) or toponym (e.g. *pontes*).[70] Most commonly, however, hydronyms are treated indistinguishably from toponyms. Thus, for example, in the route from Andematunnum (Langres) to Tullum (Toul), the river Mosa (Meuse) is cited in no different fashion to a town or village (385, 6-10):

... ab Andemantunno Tullo Leucorum usque m.p. XLIII:
Mosa   m.p. XII
Solimariaca   m.p. XVI
Tullum   m.p. XV

In such cases there is potential for confusion where a river shares its name with a settlement. For example, in the direct overland route described from Catina (Catania) on Sicily's east coast to Agrigentum (Agrigento) on its south-western shore, the station 'Gela siue Filosofianis' (88, 2) refers to the route's crossing of the river Gela (Nociara) near Philosophiana (Piazza Armerina) rather than to passing through the city of Gela on the coast 18 miles to the south. That most rivers are noted in this fashion, as stages without further comment, suggests that they could be crossed without fuss by bridge or ford.

Some rivers were sufficiently broad to require a ferry crossing (*traiectus*) and, as such, they are immortalised in the toponymy recorded. Perhaps the most famous is the *traiectus* (sc. *Rheni*, i.e. Utrecht: 369, 2) noted on the route from Lugdunum *caput Germaniarum* (Leiden) to Argentorate (Strasbourg). A *traiectus* of eight miles is recorded over the Severn Estuary (486, 2: *m.p. VIII*) as part of a route from Isca (Caerleon) in Wales to Calleua Atrebatum (Silchester) via Aquae Sulis (Bath). On a more modest scale a *trauectus* appears as a stage on the route from Aginnum (Agen) to Argentomagus (Argen-

---

[70] *Ad pontem* (409, 2; 477, 7); *pontibus* (363, 1; 478, 4).

ton-sur-Creuse), which must be at a ferry crossing of the river Dordogne (491, 9). A similar case is the *mutatio treiecto* noted by the Bordeaux traveller in the journey from Thessalonica in Macedonia to Aulon in Epirus that must represent a ferry crossing of the river Genusus (Shkumbin) encountered in the course of the Via Egnatia (*Itinerarium Burdigalense* 608, 1).

A number of ferry crossings over stretches of sea played a crucial role as nodes in the route network. For instance, the crossing at the Straits of Messina from the toe of Italy to Sicily features prominently (86, 3: *a traiecto Lilybaeo m.p. CCLVII*; 98, 4-5: *iter quod a Mediolano ...ad columnam, id est traiectum Siciliae, ducit m.p. DCCCCS*; 106, 5: *ab Urbe recto itinere ad Columnam m.p. CCCCLV*). Also featured are the *traiectum Asiae* or *traiectus in Asia* from Callipolis (Gelibolu) to Lampsacus (Lapseki) (333, 2; 333, 9-10: *stadia LX*), the crossing of the Thracian Bosporus from Byzantium to Chalcedon is recorded as four miles (139, 1-2: *m.p. IIII*), and, most importantly, the crossing of the Ionian Sea from southern Italy to Epirus (115, 7-8: *ab Aequo Tutico Hydrunto ad traiectum m.p. CCXXXV*; 317, 5-6: *a Brundisio traiectus Durrachium usque stadia num. Ī CCCC*; 323, 9-10: *a Brundisio siue ab Hydrunto traiectus Aulonam stadia num. Ī*; 329, 1-2: *recto itinere ab Hydrunti Aulonam stadia Ī*); the last two of which were made by the 'Bordeaux traveller'.[71] In fact, this traveller recorded the precise dates of his/her two Bosporan crossings (30 May and 26 December AD 333 respectively) and also made a note of the length in stades of the Aulon-Hydruntum crossing, even if this survives only in a rather garbled form. Other crossings featured in the *Itinerarium Antonini* are the *traiectus* of the *sinus Liburnicus* (Riječki zaljev), which provides a short cut from Pola in Istria to Iader (Zadar) in Dalmatia (272, 1-2: *stadia CCCCL*) and that across the English Channel from Gesoriacum (Boulogne) *in Gallis* to Rutupiae (Richborough),

---

[71] *Itinerarium Burdigalense* 571, 6-10: *Item ambulauimus Dalmati{c}o et Zenophilo cons. III kal. Iun. a Calcedonia et reuersi sumus Constantinopolim VII kal. Ian. cons. suprascripto. A Constantinopoli transis Pontum, uenis Calcedoniam, ...*; 608, 10-609, 5: *mansio Aulona treiectum* (sic) *... trans mare stadia mille, quod facit milia centum, et uenis Odronto.*

the *portus Britanniarum* (463, 4-5: *stadia CCCCL*). Although not universally true, it is notable that most of the journeys across open water are
measured in stades rather than miles, in contrast to the proportions
for the coasting or 'tramping' routes, where miles predominate.

On the other hand there are not infrequent instances where a *traiectus* that must have been made is not noted. For instance, even such
a significant crossing as that of the Thracian Bosporus escapes mention in the itinerary from Viminacium (Kostolac) on the Danube to
Nicomedia (İzmit) in Bithynia. This jumps from Byzantium on the
European side (230, 11) to Pantichium (Pendik) on the gulf of
Nicomedia (231, 1), without even mentioning the change of continents. That the distance is not even accounted for suggests that the
traiectus has dropped out. Similarly though, on a smaller scale, the
route northwards from Athens to Thessaly crosses from Oropos and
Thebes in Boeotia to Chalcis in Euboea and back again, without ever
noting that it has left the mainland, though admittedly this involves
only a very short hop across the Euripus.

As well as the traversing of rivers and straits there was, of course,
always the option of taking a riverboat down- or even upstream along
the length of a river. In some cases, such as the Nile in Egypt, taking
the river would be the obvious and normal choice for long-distance
travel. After all, since the desert restricted all major settlement to the
river's banks, the Nile was the natural artery of communication. The
travel accounts of one Theophanes and his party from Hermopolis
on the Nile to Antioch in Syria c. AD 320 demonstrate this well.[72] He
began by taking a boat down the Nile to Alexandria and then made
his way on by road across the delta, most likely making use of the
public post (*cursus publicus*) that was available to official travellers. The
Nile was, in fact, blessed by the double advantage of the current flowing from south to north and a prevailing wind in the opposite direc-

---

[72] *P.Ryl.* IV 627-8, 638; B.R. Rees, "Theophanes of Hermopolis Magna",
BRL 51 (1968) 164-183; Casson, *Travel* 190-193; C.E.P. Adams, "'There
and back again': Getting around in Roman Egypt", in idem & Laurence
(edd.), *Travel and Geography* 159-162.

tion; boats could float downstream and sail upstream.[73] Given this
fortunate set of circumstances, one might expect the routes offered
by the *Itinerarium Antonini* to reflect use of the waterway. However, its
routes southwards from Alexandria to Hierasycaminos (154.5-162.4)
and back northwards up to the delta (164, 1-170, 4) adhere strictly to
stations entirely on the west bank and east bank respectively (cf. the
Tabula Peutingeriana below). A true riverine itinerary would more naturally indicate each town in sequence irrespective of which side of the
Nile they are located. Not that the possibilities of travel by fresh-
water are ignored entirely in the collection. In two routes down from
the Alps to Milan, one is advised to travel *per lacum* down the length of
Lake Como (277, 4; 278, 7-279, 1). By analogy might the formula *per
ripam* used elsewhere hint at the possibility of riverine travel, as, perhaps, a fresh-water equivalent of the phrase *per loca maritima*? Does this
phrase mean travelling on land 'on the bank' or by water 'along the
bank'? The details of the stations associated with the route *per ripam*
(sc. of the Euphrates) from Melitene to Samosata (207, 10) are incon-
clusive. In the case of the itinerary *per ripam a Viminacio ad Nicomediam*
(217, 5-6), which follows the south bank of the Danube all the way to
its mouth, the phrase is implicitly contrasted with an overland route
that would take the traveller directly south-east across Moesia and
Thrace to Byzantium, as outlined as part of the continuous itinerary
from Rome to Hierasycaminos (133, 3-138, 5). A contrast is explicit in
the detailing of the routes from Pannonia to Gaul either *per mediter-
ranea loca* (i.e. 'inland places': 231, 8-9) or *per ripam* (sc. *Danubii et Rheni*:
241, 1-2) but this does not help resolve the problem of whether the
latter phrase implies a route involving riverine travel or not. Perhaps
the distinction is, after all, false. For, where a road ran alongside a navigable river, the choice of land or water transport would be the traveller's rather than being dictated by the route-plan, which would, in
fact, be equally applicable whichever option was taken. In reality this
choice might be dependent on a number of variables. While it was no

[73] On which see Casson, *Travel* 257-258.

doubt easier to take a journey downstream on the water, it might be easier to do the opposite journey by land; a clause from the water-transport appendix of Diocletian's Price Edict of AD 301 considers transport upstream as generally twice as costly as that downstream.[74] Alternatively, the option might only be seasonably available; a river navigable in winter, when roads were inhospitable, might dry to a mere trickle in the summer months.[75] Accordingly, a reasonable interpretation is that the appearance of the phrase *per ripam* in the description of a route indicates that travel by riverboat might be an option for at least part of the journey contemplated.

3.1.b) The *itinerarium maritimum*

The *itinerarium maritimum* begins with the ambitiously programmatic statement that, 'beginning from Gades or the extreme edge of Africa, it auspiciously instructs what shores one sailing ought to know to stick to or to go by'.[76] This is reminiscent of the opening of the preceding *itinerarium prouinciarum*, suggesting that the compiler of the *Itinerarium Antonini* was striving to impose a uniform structure upon his provincial and maritime itineraries. However, this statement would seem to reflect the compiler's aspiration rather than actual achievement. For, despite this claim to comprehensiveness, the maritime itinerary is an even more heterogeneous, patchy, and disjointed document than

---

[74] J.M. Reynolds in C.M Roueché, *Aphrodisias in Late Antiquity* (JRS Monograph 5, London 1989) 307, chap. 35A [now Chap. 70 according to the re-edition by M.H. Crawford in R.R.R. Smith et al., *Aphrodisias. The Basilica*, forthcoming], lines 31-32, [*pe*]*r mi*[*li*]*a pass*[*us XX* ƒ]*luuium aqua discendentis per singulos modios X unum | [aqua asc*]*end*[*entis per*] *milia passus XX per singulos mo*(*dios*) *X duos*: 'for each modius descending a river by water for 20 miles, 1 denarius; for each modius ascending by water for twenty miles, 2 denarii'.

[75] Laurence, *Roads of Roman Italy*, 109-114.

[76] 487, 3-4: ... *itinerarium maritimum, ut nauigans qua litora tenens nosse debeat aut qua ambire, incipiens a Gadibus uel extrema Africa perdocet feliciter*.

the provincial one, and might justifiably be called a miscellany. Four distinct subsections can be discerned, each belonging to a different genre and exhibiting a different style. The first is a *periplus* of the *from X to Y, stades Z* type, similar in structure to Menippus and the anonymous *Stadiasmus* (487, 4-493, 11); the second is a list of crossings (*traiectus*) in the Atlantic and western Mediterranean, again measured in stades (493, 12-497, 8); the third is a coastal itinerary in miles listing the harbours and anchorages from Rome to Arelate (Arles) on the Rhône in southern Gaul (497, 9-508, 2); and the fourth is a very uneven catalogue of islands in the Atlantic and Mediterranean, with distances from the shore or each other indicated once again in stades (508, 3-529, 6).

Following directly after the programmatic heading, the opening *periplus* immediately disappoints expectations because, instead of outlining a route from the Pillars of Hercules, it opens with 'those places that you have to touch upon when you begin to sail from the province of Achaea (Greece) via Sicily to Africa'.[77] There follow the details of a shore-hugging voyage from the Corinthian gulf to Africa by following the coast of Epirus northwards up to Aulon, then turning westwards to make the short crossing (*traiectus*) of the Ionian Sea to Hydruntum (Otranto) in Calabria, then turning southwards following the coast (*litoraria* sc. *per loca*) to Leuca (Capo Sta Maria di Leuca), sailing direct from there southwestwards across the Gulf of Tarentum to Croton, and then following the coast around to the Straits of Messina. Rather than attempting to fight against the current of the Straits, the itinerary follows Sicily's east and south shores around to its westernmost point at Lilybaeum (Marsala), then out to the outlying island of Maritima (Marettimo), which forms the jumping-off point for several different *traiectus* to the north-east coast of modern Tunisia and a final destination in Carthage on the Gulf of Tunis or Hadru-

---

[77] 487, 4-5: *Incipit: Quae loca tangere debeas cum nauigare ceperis ex prouincia Achaia per Siciliam ad Africam usque*; a sentence that may have grown up to explain the abrupt disjunction between title and contents (see Cuntz's apparatus *ad loc.*)

metum on the Gulf of Hammamet. Overall, then, this is inadequate to the description in two respects: firstly, by progressing from east to west, rather than west to east; and secondly in getting no closer to the Pillars of Hercules than Carthage. The acute reader of the collection might make good the deficiency in part by recalling the advice to sail along the coast from Tingis (Tangiers) to Portus Diuinus (Rade de Mers el Kébir) from the first section of the provincial itinerary (9, 1-13, 7), though this would still leave the remaining 894 Roman miles to Carthage undescribed.

As befitting contemporary nautical practice, at no point is an open sea journey of more than a thousand stades involved. The itinerary also provides orientation details with reference to terrestrial landmarks similar in nature to those found in Menippus and the *Stadiasmus*. An example is the detailed instruction on the location of the *insula Sassonis* (Sazan) that provides the jumping-off point for the crossing to Hydruntum: 'From Buthrotum to the Island of Sazan in the above-mentioned province [Epirus Vetus], beyond (*super*) Acroceraunia [kepi i Gjuhezës], ... one leaves Aulon to the right on the shoreward side' (see below).[78] Even so, without any indication of bearing, it would still be hard to steer an accurate course for the heel of Italy on this basis. One relative bearing of some practical use is provided: the comment that the alternative to the Sicily-Carthage crossing is 'to steer a course *superius* towards Libya.'[79] Uggeri has argued that both these directional indications (*super*/*superius*) result from the derivation of the itinerary from navigational charts; though since these indications point in opposite directions (north in the first case, south in the latter), he postulates charts orientated to opposite compass points.[80] However, the contradiction might be resolved, if the indications are related to

---

[78] On the role of Cassiope on Cercyra (Corfù) and the little island of Sason (Sazan) as landmarks for navigation of the Epirus-Calabria crossing see Marangio in Laudizi & Marangio (edd.), *Porti, approdi e linee di rotta* 79-104.

[79] 493, 4-7: *si autem non Carthaginem sed superius ad Libyam uersus uolueris adplicare, debes uenire de Sicilia ab insula Maritima in promunturium Mercurii.*

[80] Uggeri in Laudizi & Marangio (edd.), *Porti, approdi e linee di rotta* 51-52.

the prevailing currents and winds in each case; *super Acroceraunia* ('downstream/downwind') would indeed take you north to Sazan and, likewise, turning to steer a course *superius* ('further downstream/ downwind') would take you southeast from Marettimo to the Gulf of Syrtis (see fig. 8).

However, on the whole the *itinerarium maritimum* is less detailed than its Greek counterparts and provides no information on the location and quality of harbours, anchorages, etc., and is missing the summary totals of distances that are one of the distinctive structural features of the Greek *periplus* writers. On the other hand, it exhibits a novel, and almost obsessive, concern to identify the precise Roman province to which each location belongs, perhaps originating in some bureaucratic purpose. This can be illustrated from the opening section (488, 1-489, 8):

Ab Istmo Naupactum usque prouinciae Achaiae	stadia DCCL
a Naupacto Oxeas prouinciae Epiri Veteris	stadia CCCC
ab Oxeis Nicopoli prouinciae supra scriptae	stadia DCC
a Nicopoli Butroto prouinciae supra scriptae	stadia D
a Buthroto Sassonis insula prouinciae supra scriptae super Acroceraunia, et relinquit Aulonam in dextro interius	stadia C
a Sassonis insula traiectus Hidrunto prouinciae Calabriae	stadia CCCC
ab Ydrunti litoraria Leucas prouinciae supra scriptae	stadia CCC
a Leucis Crotona prouinciae <supra scriptae>	stadia DCCC

Given that the surviving sections of the *Stadiasmus* provide an itinerary anticlockwise from Alexandria as far as Attica and the Argolid and clockwise as far as Utica, with just a slight gap in Greece and a slight overlap around Carthage, this almost exactly complements the *Stadiasmus* to complete a *periplus* of the eastern basin of the Mediterranean (fig. 9).

The second section comprises a list of sixteen *traiectus* between various points in the western Mediterranean and Adriatic, as well as the Boulogne to Richborough crossing of the English Channel (493, 12-

497, 8). Again the distances, as appropriate to measurements across open sea, are given in stades. The longest crossing quoted is the first, and perhaps most important, that from the Portus Augusti (Porto) at Rome to Carthage, at 5,250 stades. None of the rest exceeds 3,000 stades, there being two of this distance: Caralis (Cagliari) in Sardinia to Portus (494, 3-4) and Carthago Spartaria (Cartagena) to Caesarea Mauretania (Cherchel) (496, 1-2). The next longest are three of 1,500 stades: that from Caralis to Carthage (494, 5-6) and two quoted for different crossings of the Adriatic (497, 3, 8). Structurally, this section is most similar to that section of the *Stadiasmus* that lists point-to-point distances from Cos/Myndos and Delos to various locations in the eastern Mediterranean (*Stad.* 274-79, 284).

However, what follows is quite different. It is described as an itinerary of the ports and anchorages for ships (*itinerarium portuum uel positionum nauium*) from Rome to Arles and indeed lists the nature of the stages in considerably greater detail than the preceding sections. Rather like the north African section of the *Stadiasmus*, as well as harbours (*portus*) and anchorages (*positiones*), at Albintimilium (Ventimiglia), Nicaea (Nice), and the sinus Sambracitanus (golfe de Saint Tropez), beaches (*plagiae*) are noted, as they are in the Sicilian section of the *itinerarium prouinciarum* (95, 2-96, 4; see above).[81] Such information is, of course, most useful for shipping 'tramping' up the coast, as Rutilius Namatianus did along this very route. In contrast to the preceding sections this coastal route gives the measurements in miles rather than stades. The style is illustrated by the final section from Forum Iulii (Fréjus) to Arles (505, 2-508, 2):

a Foro Iuli sinus Sambracitanus, plagia,	m.p. XXV
a sinu Sambracitano Heraclia Caccabaria, portus,	m.p. XVI
ab Heraclia Caccabaria Alconis, portus,	m.p. XII
ab Alconis Pomponianis, portus,	m.p. XXX
a Pomponianis Telone Martio, portus,	m.p. XVIII

[81] R. Uggeri, "La terminologia portuale romana e la documentazione dell'Itinerarium Antonini", *Studi Italiani di Filologia Classica* 40 (1968) 225-254.

a Telone Martio Taurento, portus,	m.p. XII
a Taurento Carsicis, portus,	m.p. XII
a Carsicis Citarista, portus,	m.p. XVIII
a Citarista portus Hemines, positio,	m.p. VI
a portu Aemines Inmadras, positio,	m.p. XII
ab Inmadris Masilia Grecorum, portus,	m.p. XII
a Masilia Grecorum Incaro, positio,	m.p. XII
ab Incaro Dilis, positio,	m.p. VIII
a Dilis Fossis Marianis, portus,	m.p. XII
a Fossis ad Gradum Massilitanorum, fluuius Rhodanus,	m.p. XVI
a Gradu per fluuium Rhodanum Arelatum,	m.p. XXX

The qualifications *portus, positio,* etc. stand out, as nominatives, distinct from the generally oblique cases of the toponyms that grammatically form part of the main sentence of the list. While these qualifications may derive from glosses made by a traveller on the archetype of this list, they are as easily understood as an ellipsis for a relative clause (i.e., for example, 'from the sinus Sambracitanus to Heraclia Caccabaria, which is a port, 16 miles'). The level of detail and figures in miles rather than stades have led some to see this section as an extract from 'official' files, though opinion diverges widely on its date. René Lugand preferred to put it in the later first century AD (after Nero), while Uggeri dates it to between the mid fifth and sixth centuries, on the basis of the presence of the toponym *Portus Maurici* (Porto Maurizio-Impéria: 503, 1) and that of *Gradus*, rather than *Ostium Massilitanorum* (Crau: 507, 7-508, 1), and he also sees the coverage of the entire maritime section of the *Itinerarium Antonini* as reflecting Vandal interests.[82] However, while *gradus* ('step', 'platform', 'flats', 'landing stage'; cf. Grado di Aquileia and the connotations of modern Italian *scalo*) does have a later Latin air to it, without the designation '*Sancti* Maurici' there is no reason to link the toponym of Porto Maurizio to the

---

[82] R. Lugand, "Note sur l'itineraire maritime de Rome à Arles", *MEFRA* 43 (1926) 124-139; Uggeri, *Studi Italiani di Filologia Classica* 40 (1968) 225-254; idem in Laudizi & Marangio (edd.), *Porti, approdi e linee di rotta* 53-58.

fifth-century spread of the cult of Saint Maurice nor to push the date
of this section any later than the fourth century.

The final section is made up of a series of lists of islands, working
eastwards from the Atlantic, beginning with those that are 'in the
Ocean that flows between Gaul and Britain', which, although linked
to the preceding sections by *item* (similarly), does not naturally form
part of a grammatical unit with them.[83] Moreover, this section is
rather uneven in quality. The islands in the North Atlantic are simply
listed, whereas those in the western Mediterranean basin are also
located by distances (in stades) from each other or from some point
on the mainland. East of Sicily, only the islands of the Adriatic down
to Cassiope (the town on Corfù) are located by distances (519, 3-521,
3), even if rather misleadingly titled 'inter Dalmatiam et Histriam'
(519, 3). In fact, the quality of this description is symptomatic of the
poorer standard of the information for the eastern Mediterranean.
The Ionian islands are marooned without distances or a separate
heading in a list appended to the list of islands 'inter Siciliam et Africam' (519, 1-2); and, under the heading 'in the sea that flows between
Thrace and Crete', are listed locations in the northern Aegean, most
but not all of them islands, Eretria and Chalcis, for example, being
cities on the island of Euboea (521, 4-523, 2). This is followed,
without warning, by a list of islands linked with mythological events,
ordered roughly west to east, from the Strophades and the Ionian
islands to Cyprus (523, 3-526, 1). Thus we are told that Ithaca was the
homeland of Ulysses (524, 3), that Juno was born on Samos (524, 4),
and that Cyprus is consecrated to Venus (526, 1). This is interrupted
by the confused heading that 'Similarly in the Hellespont are the
islands of the Cyclades, located between the Aegean and Malean sea,
and surrounded also by the Myrtoan sea' (526, 3-5), under which are
listed various of the Cyclades and Dodecanese, with some repetition
from the section on the sea between Thrace and Crete.[84] Many of

---

[83]   508, 3-4: *Item in mari oceano, quod Gallias et Britannias interluit.*
[84]   E.g. Scyros and Andros: 527, 7 and 529, 2; cf. 523, 1 and 522, 2.

these also have information of a largely mythological character attached. For example, Naxos is described as the island on which 'Ariadne, having been abandoned by Theseus, was loved by Bacchus' (528, 2-3). The only information that could conceivably be of any practical use are the two isolated figures given for the distance between Myconos and Delos and Myconos and Icaria, and the description of Paros as the island in which 'the most dazzling white stone originates' (527, 5-6; 527, 8).

In all, even with the information of its disparate sections combined, the *itinerarium maritimum* falls far short of being a comprehensive description of the Roman-controlled seas. The imbalance in length between the provincial and maritime parts of the *Itinerarium Antonini* is striking (in the Teubner edition, seventy-five pages as compared with ten). One could legitimately argue that there are naturally fewer itinerary stages to be noted for the maritime sphere (essentially only islands and coastal locations) – the bulk of the sea being an indistinguishable mass – than for the land, where more or less its entire depth is dotted with towns and other significant nuclei of human society to which routes might be described. On the other hand, given the infinite pathlessness of the sea, the systematic listing of coastal ports and detailing of distances to potential destinations therefrom might require just as much, if not more, description than listing the relatively finite number of routes out of each town; not to mention detailing the courses of navigable rivers, the nearest equivalent to terrestrial routes. The potential level of detail possible is suggested by the final chapter of Diocletian's Prices Edict, which listed the maximum fees for cargoes between major destinations and which would originally have listed forty-nine point-to-point journeys.[85] That this itself was considered far from comprehensive is indicated by the

---

[85] M.H. Crawford & J.M. Reynolds, "The Aezani Copy of the Prices Edict", *ZPE* 34 (1979), 184-186, chap. 35 [now Chap. 69 according to the re-edition by Crawford in R.R.R. Smith et al., *Aphrodisias. The Basilica*, forthcoming]: *ex quibus locis ad quas prouincias quantum nau<a>li excedere minime sit licitum.*

appending of a chapter of *addenda* of unknown length.[86] The relative
deficiency of the maritime itinerary is probably attributable to the
inaccessibility of data to the compiler. As noted, the overall organisation of the *Itinerarium Antonini* suggests a western-based, if not Spanish
or Mauretanian compiler. It is not surprising, then, that the western
Mediterranean basin is most thoroughly described; but even here, the
only detailed coastal description provided is the 'tramping' route from
Rome to Arles, whose distances in miles suggest that it was from the
first composed in Latin. Moreover, the increasingly vague nature of
the information provided as the survey of islands progresses eastward,
suggests that a probably Greekless compiler was dependent on what
information he could find in translation, which for the Aegean and
eastern Mediterranean might be nothing more than a commentary on
Homeric geography. A language barrier may not have been the only,
or even major problem, however. Given the overall imbalance in survival of terrestrial as compared with maritime itineraries and the lesser
public demand for the latter, it is possible that fewer circulated in
written form. After all, though less extreme, a mirror image of the
patchiness of the maritime part of the *Itinerarium Antonini* has been
observed in the coverage of the naval cargo chapter of the Prices
Edict. This may reflect reliance by its compilers on the local knowledge of the sailors to whom they had access (perhaps in Syrian
Antioch).[87]

---

[86] Chap. 35A [70 Crawford]; for which Reynolds in Roueché, *Aphrodisias*
306-311.

[87] M.K. Hopkins, "The transport of staples", in *Eighth International Economic
History Congress, Budapest 1982* (Budapest 1982), 80-87, esp. table 1, 85-86;
idem, "Models, ships, and staples", in P.D.A. Garnsey & C.R. Whittaker
(edd.), *Trade and Famine in Classical Antiquity* (Cambridge Philological
Society suppl. 8, Cambridge 1983) 102-104; S.J.J. Corcoran, *The Empire of
the Tetrarchs: Imperial Pronouncements and Government AD 284-324,* rev. ed.
(Oxford 2000) 224-225.

3.2 The *Tabula Peutingeriana*

This unique document, comprising a series of eleven parchment leaves, 6.75 m long by 32-24 cm high, bears a squashed and elongated depiction of the entire known world (*oecumene*), though the most westerly portion, containing most of Britain, Spain, and Mauretania, is now lost. The surviving artefact is a manuscript of probably late twelfth- or early thirteenth-century date with a probable provenance in the zone of the upper reaches of the Rhine and Danube.[88] However, although composed of geographical material of even more disparate date than the *Itinerarium Antonini*, the *Tabula Peutingeriana* would appear to be a more-or-less faithful copy of an original whose contents can be put no earlier than the mid fourth century AD but which might have been drafted at any point thereafter. Although much remains controversial about its origins, it appears to have been produced by mapping out the data of an itinerary collection akin to the *Itinerarium Antonini* onto a graphic depiction of the *oecumene*.[89] On this the sea is depicted in a green pigment, leaving the land represented by the natural brown colour of the vellum. On the land, the routes from the itineraries are represented by straight lines in red ink, punctuated by jagged kinks to indicate way-stations (named in black ink) and occasionally interrupted by little 'icons' or vignettes representing significant towns, temples, bath-complexes, etc. If the paucity of the maritime section of the *Itinerarium Antonini* is representative, given that the *Tabula* too is almost certainly a private production, it comes as no surprise to find that there is no network of coasting routes or sea crossings drawn over the seas equivalent to that on land. There are, nevertheless, indications that at least some data deriving from mari-

---

[88] Vienna, Österreichische Nationalbibliothek, ms. lat. 324.

[89] On the nature of the *Tabula Peutingeriana* see Salway in Adams & Laurence, *Travel and Geography* 22-23, 28-32, 43-47; Whittaker in McKechnie (ed.), *Thinking Like a Lawyer* 93-95, 105-106, 109-110; and Talbert in this volume. – In this article, references to the *Tabula* follow the system devised by Weber (on which see Talbert in this volume pp. 140-141).

time itineraries has contributed to the information displayed. As well as one sea crossing, the *Tabula* includes some small islands and coastal features that appear elsewhere as significant points for navigation. Also, at least one river and one maritime route have been represented as part of the terrestrial network, the former explicitly, the latter apparently inadvertently.

3.2.a) The Rivers

In general it seems likely that the rivers and lakes depicted on the *Tabula Peutingeriana* derive, like the mountains, regional and tribal names, and the outline of the seas and continents, from a graphic representation of the *oecumene*. Just as the drafter distorted the geography in order to fit the long thin format, so the courses of rivers have naturally also been distorted. Accordingly, the drafter could only bring the rivers into relation with his route network when the terrestrial itinerary mentioned a river crossing. Apart from the elaborate vignettes for Rome and Antioch, incorporating the Tiber and Orontes, the only examples of rivers being drawn through towns are Aosta (*Augusta Pretoria*: II 4 m), Fusṭāṭ near Cairo (*Babilonia*: VIII 4 u), and Babylon (*Babylonia*: X 4 u). Beyond this, the depiction of the rivers is best described as impressionistic.[90] Nevertheless, it is tempting to see in the rubrication along the banks of many rivers in Gaul, Germany, and northern Italy, which is such a striking feature of Konrad Miller's colour apograph edition of 1888,[91] the drafter's attempt to represent, with the same colour that he used for land routes, an *itinerarium fluuiale*. The argument seems to gain further weight from the fact that the coast around the western end of Sicily gets the same treatment,

---

[90] R. Barginesi, "L'idrografia padana in alcune rappresentazioni antiche", *Geographia Antiqua* 8-9 (1999-2000) 117-118, citing his own "Il bacino del Po nella Tabula Peutingeriana", Συγγραφή 1 (1998) 143-154 (non vidi).

[91] K. Miller, *Die Weltkarte des Castorius genannt die Peutingersche Tafel* (Ravensburg 1888); on which see Talbert in this volume.

roughly from Thermae Himeraeae (Termini Imerese) to Aquae Laro-
des (V 5 m - VI 1 m); precisely the area that is covered by routes *per
loca maritima* in the *Itinerarium Antonini* (90, 6-93, 1; 97, 7-98, 1). However, despite the fact that some of the rivers that are rubricated all or
in part were famously navigable, such as the Moselle (II 1 o), the
Rhine (II 4 o), and the Po (II 3 m- IV 1 m), this is less clearly the case
for various rivers in Liguria and northern Etruria (II 3 m - III 4 m).
Moreover, it is less obvious from the facsimile edition that this
rubrication has such a specific purpose. It seems better to ascribe its
presence or absence to the vagaries of the drafter or later copyists.

Nevertheless, there is one certain example of a river route, though
graphically it is treated exactly as if it were a road. This is the label *ab
Hostilia per Padum*, on a route starting at Verona, attached to a straight
red line linking Hostilia (Ostiglia) directly with Ravenna without any
intermediate stations or distances (III 5 m; fig. 10). The absence of
any measure of distance, if not simply a scribal oversight, contrasts
with the identically phrased preceding stretch, and may suggest the
switch from easily measurable public road, equipped with milestones,
to meandering featureless waterway.[92] As a land route Hostilia to Ravenna is implausible, and certainly no Roman highway is known
archaeologically to traverse this terrain in this direction. On the other
hand it is perfectly explicable as a river route. Hostilia seems to have
been the *caput uiae* for the via Claudia Augusta, running northwards to
Verona and over the Alps, linking the Po with the Danube.[93] Hostilia
is the point where the route south intersects with the Po, so that a
traveller making for Ravenna from Verona would be well advised to
embark at this point and follow the Po along one of its branches to
the Adriatic coast. In fact, by taking the most southerly branch and
the artificial Fossa Augusta, the traveller could stay on a riverboat all

[92] Verona – a Verona Hostilia milia passus xxxiii – Hostiliae – ab Hostilia
per Padum – Rauenna (III 4 m-IV 1 m).

[93] *CIL* V 8003; S. Patitucci, "I porti fluviali nell'Italia padana tra Antichità e
Altomedioevo", in Laudizi & Marangio (edd.), *Porti, approdi e linee di rotta*
259-260.

the way to his destination, as did the poet, statesman, and later bishop, Sidonius Apollinaris, arriving there in the mid-fifth century from Gaul.[94] Without the clue 'per Padum' it would be all to easy to assume that this route represented a road, so that it is quite possible that other riverine routes do lie undetected elsewhere on the *Tabula*. This may be the case for the rather confused route shown following the Nile southwards, which links sites on both banks along a single road, as well as being shown inaccurately crossing the river at one point (VIII 1-3 u).

3.2.b) The Sea

By and large the terrestrial network is not linked into the coastline, which is generally indicated by an undifferentiated wavy line. While the vignettes for a number of towns are made to sit upon the coastline, in most cases nothing is made of their status as ports from which the traveller might take to the sea.[95] The Dalmatian coast presents a localised exception to this because, on at least four occasions, towns near the coast are attributed corresponding labels in the sea denoting them as *portus*.[96] Still, no special symbol is used to denote these ports and, in fact, the coastline is only individualised at four points throughout the entire *Tabula*: the Mediterranean end of the Pyrenean chain, labelled in the sea *promunturium Pyreneum* (I 2 m); some cliffs also labelled in the sea *in alpe maritima* (II 3 m); Portus Augusti at Rome (IV 5 m); and the Pharos at Alexandria (VIII 3 u). Although these first two are not linked by lines of red ink to the route network, they are correctly positioned in relation to stages named on terrestrial routes (*in summo Pyreneo*; *in alpe maritima*). Portus and Alexandria, on the other

---

[94] Sidonius, *Ep.* 1.5; Laurence, *Roads of Roman Italy* 115-119.
[95] E.g. Narbo Martius (*Narbone*: I 3 m), Ostia (*Hostis*: IV 5 m) and Syracusae (*Siracusis*: VI 2 u).
[96] [Flanona]: *portus Flanaticus* (IV 1 o); Senia: *portus Senia* (IV 2 o); Salona: *portus <S>alonitanus* (V 3 o); Epetio: *portus Epetius* (V 3 o).

hand, have both lost their labels but are (or were originally) linked in as nodes on the terrestrial route network and are, significantly, represented by unique symbols, representing the famous port facilities and lighthouse respectively.[97] Their special treatment is noteworthy in the light of their status as the termini of the direct sea route from Rome to Alexandria.

These two locations aside, there are only a few places where a rubricated route ends on the coastline itself. The only one of these in which there is any real possibility that it is a deliberate attempt to represent a transfer to travel by sea *per loca maritima* is after 'Cesernia' on the route running northwards along the Lucanian coast from Vibo Valentia (VI 1 m). Although the red line ends abruptly at the coastline, the next stage up the coast, Paestum, is labelled with a distance (*Pestu(m) xxxuii*: V 5 m-VI 1 m) and the facing stretch of water is correspondingly labelled *Sinus Pestanus* (V 5 m). There is a similar lacuna in the land route to the other side of Paestum until the next stage, Salernum (*Salerno ix*: V 5 m), from which two routes are shown heading inland. Given the topography of this coastline, alternately rugged and marshy, it is not implausible that the route advised taking to 'tramping' vessels for this stretch. Nevertheless, we should always bear in mind the simple explanation that the copyist has failed to draw in the red line for the route, as has happened frequently elsewhere.

The opposite phenomenon, where a route that can only logically be one taken by sea is indicated as a terrestrial route, is to be found in the Asia Minor section. Here a route is drawn from Miletus in Ionia to Patara in Lycia, via Myndos, Cnidos, and Loryma (*Miletum lui* – *Mindo fl.* [sic] *xxuii* – *Chidum lxx* – *Lorimna lxii* – *Patras*: IX 1-2 m). Comparison with the real geography of the region reveals that Myndos, Cnidos, and Loryma sit at the end of long (and in the latter

---

[97] Beneath the Pharos icon, there is a blank space abutted by abruptly ending roads from Taposiris on the left and Hermopolis on the right (VIII 3 u). There is a similar, though less elaborate, symbol to that for Portus at Fossae Marianae (*Fossis Marianis*: I 5 m) in southern Gaul, but it does not interrupt the coastline in the same fashion.

two cases also fairly inaccessible) peninsulas and that these are separated from each other and Miletus and Patara by extensive gulfs (see fig. 11). Thus this makes no sense as a land route. Presumably the textual itinerary from which the drafter was working simply listed these places with intermediate distances in miles, without any hint that it was a 'tramping' route rather than a road that was being followed. Alternatively, through lack of attentiveness or knowledge of the genuine geography of the area, the drafter failed to realise the implications of a *per loca maritima* rubric.

The one *traiectus* that is featured on the *Tabula* may derive from a list similar to that in the maritime section of the *Itinerarium Antonini,* but might equally well have been embedded in a terrestrial itinerary. It is indicated simply by a label in the sea in the Laconic Gulf of the Peloponnese, which baldly states *traiectus stadior(um) CC,* without specifying its termini (VII 1 m). The distance could equally well refer to a crossing from Gythium (*Cytnion*) to the island of Cythera (*ins. Cytera:* VII 2 m), or to the more significant one from Boeae (*Boas,* i.e. Neapolis) to the western end of Crete (VII 5 m).

As noted above, there is a cluster of detail for ports along the Dalmatian coast. In fact there is a general concentration of labels in the sea and for islands down the length of the Adriatic, into the Ionian sea, and round the bottom of Italy to Sicily that suggests a coasting itinerary as the source linking these notices, though the accuracy with which they are handled declines as the Adriatic is descended. For, while the Istrian peninsula (IV 1 o), the promontories of Zara (*Iadera:* IV 3 o) and Trogir (*Tragurium:* V 3 o), and the bay of Solin (*Salona:* V 3 o) are represented with some resemblance to geographical reality, the drafter seems to have lost his touch not much further south. Thus the nearby islands of Corcyra Nigra (Korčula) and Melita (Mljet) are dislocated a long way to the right (south), to some point opposite Brundisium (Brindisi) (VI 1 o). Real confusion begins as one enters the Ionian sea. The point of Acroceraunia in Epirus is transformed into an island (*ins. Acrocer':* VI 2 o), while the island of Sazan, the associated landmark for the crossing to Italy, is duplicated (*ins. Sasonis:* VI 2 o, VI 3 m). The same happens to Cephalonia (VI 3 m, VI 3 u), while

Corfù features twice under different names (*ins. Crocira* [sic]: VI 2 o;
ins. Cassiopa: VI 3 u). This type of error must go back to the drafter,
who perhaps rather imperfectly combined a coasting itinerary with a
list of islands to produce this farrago. The sequence of labels
representing a coasting route then continues with *port. Salentinum* at
the heel of Italy, which is best understood as scribal error for
pro(mun)t(urium) Salentinum (i.e. Sta Maria di Leuca), *Leucopetra* (i.e.
Aspromonte, or, perhaps more precisely, Punto di Péllaro) at the toe,
and *port. Tragecynus* (sic, for *Traiectinus*) at *Messana* (Messina). The
influence of a list of islands akin to that ending the maritime part of
the *Itinerarium Antonini* may also be seen in the drafter's odd placement
of the Aegean Islands between the two arms of the Hellespont (VIII
1 m), since the *itinerarium maritimum* shares the same peculiarity, in that
it lists the Cyclades and Dodecanese under a heading implying that
they lie in the Hellespont.[98]

On the basis of the way in which river and sea routes appear in the
Tabula Peutingeriana, it seems likely that its drafter probably had access
to documents akin to the *Itinerarium Antonini*. The doublets produced
by inattentive compilation suggest that the drafter was attempting to
co-ordinate similarly heterogeneous sources. However, while their
coverage of islands is broadly comparable, the drafter of the *Tabula*
was not as well informed on sea crossings and coasting routes.

3.3 The Dura Parchment: terrestrial or maritime itinerary?

In the light of various discussions above it is worth taking another
look at the so-called 'Dura Shield'. This much-discussed scrap of
leather parchment was dug up in the 1920s in the excavations at
Dura-Europos on the Euphrates in Syria.[99] It is clearly a Roman

---

[98] *It. Ant.* 526, 3-4: *in Hellespontum insule Cyclades ...constitute.*
[99] Paris, Bibliothèque Nationale ms. graecus suppl. 1354.5, no. 5; F. Cumont,
      Fouilles de Doura-Europos (Paris 1926); Dilke, *Greek and Roman Maps* 120-
      122; R. Rebuffat, "Le Bouclier de Doura", *Syria* 63 (1986) 85-105; P.
      Arnaud, "Une deuxième lecture du Bouclier de Doura-Europos", *CRAI*

artefact and therefore belongs to the period before Dura's loss to the Persians in AD 260. The fragment, now measuring roughly 18 cm long x 6.5 cm high, is interpreted as belonging to the top right-hand quadrant of the covering of a circular shield (fig. 12). The parchment is decorated in multi-coloured paints with a design that clearly depicts water (in dark blue) on which there are ships filled with sailors occupying the left two-thirds, while a pale line describes an arc which would seem to represent coastline, since behind it, filling the right-hand third, are a series of stations represented by buildings with pale-green masonry or accompanied by a dark line indicating a river. These are labelled in Greek letters and with the toponyms given in oblique cases as follows (with orthography normalised and cases converted to nominative):

...

Odessos (Varna)	
Bizone (Čarakman nr. Kavarna)	
Callatis (Mangalia)	
Tomi (Constanţa)	mil. 33
Istros river (southern arm of Danube)[100]	mil. 40
Danubios river (northern arm of Danube)	
Tyras (Bilhorod-Dnistrovskij)	mil. 84
Borysthenes (i.e. Olbia on the Borysthenes; Parutino nr. Nikolaev)	
Chersonesos (Gurtschi nr. Sevastopol)	
Trapezus (mountain) (Krimskie gory)	
Arta (Straits of Kertsch)	

...

(1989) 373-389; K. Brodersen, *Terra Cognita. Studien zur römischen Raumerfassung* (Spudasmata 59, Hildesheim 1995, ²2003) 145-148.

[100] Though generally assumed, e.g. by Dilke, *Greek and Roman Maps* 121, to be an error for the city of Istria/Istros/Istropolis, this hypothesis is unnecessary since Strabo VII.3.13 and Pomponius Mela II.8 both call the southern branch of the river the Ister/Istros and the northern Danubius (the Rumanian Bratul Sfintu Gheorghe and Dunarea respectively).

The placenames show that the Black Sea coast from modern Bulgaria to the Crimea is being described; their oblique cases and the surviving distance figures show it to be an itinerary. Since all the surviving distances are given in miles rather than stades, it is generally taken to record a coastal road.[101] However, as we have seen, in Latin contexts miles were used alongside stades to measure maritime itineraries that shadowed the coastline. Moreover, Oswald Dilke detected the presence of a Latin stratum to the document in the transliteration of the Latin word *arta* (narrows) to indicate the Cimmerian Bosporus (Straits of Kertsch), not to mention the fact that the document was certainly produced in a Roman military context in which Latin was the official language. It may also be pertinent that the Dura parchment is not the only Greek text in which we find mileages for distances around the Black Sea. For the one place in the Greek *periplus* literature where one finds miles used is in the much later anonymous [Pseudo-Arrian], *Periplus of the Black Sea*, which gives distances in *stadioi* (stades) with equivalences in *milia passuum*.[102] Furthermore, it is hard on both topographical and historical grounds to imagine a Roman land route around the Black Sea coast beyond the Danube delta. Thus, given the central positioning of ships and the sea in the design of the parchment's decoration, and the lack of any line linking the stations along a road, the only plausible interpretation is that the Dura parchment represents a maritime itinerary. It may have commemorated a specific journey, as had Arrian's *Periplus* a century earlier; one perhaps under-

---

[101] E.g. Dilke, *Greek and Roman Maps* 121; K. Brodersen, "The presentation of geographical knowledge for travel and transport in the Roman world: *itineraria non tantum adnotata sed etiam picta*" in Adams & Laurence (edd.), *Travel and Geography* 15-16. Cf. Uggeri in Laudizi & Marangio (edd.), *Porti, approdi e linee di rotta* 68-69, who treats it as a map, which takes no account of the oblique cases of the toponyms.

[102] Anon. [Pseudo-Arrian] is no earlier than the last quarter of the sixth century and no later than its earliest manuscript: Universitätsbibliothek Heidelberg, codex Palatinus graecus 398 of the ninth century (Diller, *Minor Greek Geographers* 4, 113).

taken by a marine of the Pontic Fleet (*Classis Pontica*), who was subsequently transferred to the Euphrates.

Conclusions

Examining the Roman maritime and riverine itineraries together as a group has highlighted various aspects. Several different types of itinerary have been distinguished, catering for different audiences with different needs. The comprehensiveness and level of practical detail for the navigator present in the two *periploi* suggest an intended audience that is envisaged as actually commanding and navigating ships themselves. This is an audience that needs to know the location of dangerous rocks and supplies of fresh water, but does not need to be diverted with superfluous cultural information. Detailed descriptions of the coastline in linear fashion have a supremely practical purpose in a world where the vast majority of shipping stayed within sight of the shore and navigated by visible landmarks. Thus the *Periplus* of Menippus and the *Stadiasmus maris magni* are representatives of a body of technical literature that probably never had a very wide circulation. Although of little utility to the individual traveller, both may have been produced to meet the demands of a new breed of entrepreneur tempted to venture into longer distance maritime activity for the first time in the wake of the Augustan peace.

Although Menippus' work has suffered from accidental mutilation, it may well be that the *Stadiasmus* had already undergone a pruning process in antiquity. It is impossible now to know whether the clockwise itinerary was complete before the creation of the lacuna in which the beginning of the anticlockwise section also disappeared. Moreover, given the accidentally truncated form in which the *Stadiasmus* now ends (with the circumnavigation of Crete just completed), it is impossible to tell whether the ancestor of our only surviving manuscript had been edited down already to the most immediately useful portions in an Alexandrian context. The decline in the detail of the information between the surviving two fragments is notable. If this was true also for the missing descriptions of routes beyond Utica and the Peloponnese, the *Stadiasmus* may have reflected the usual roaming limits of the ordinary Alexandrian merchantman, rather than the long-distance bulk grain carriers. If so, this would serve to confirm Braudel's view of the two relatively exclusive halves of the Mediterranean.

Despite the wide dissemination of collections of itineraries for the independent traveller, represented by the *Itinerarium Antonini* and, at a degree removed, by the *Tabula Peutingeriana*, these clearly did not contain comprehensive details of the navigability of rivers or extensive *periploi* describing the coasting routes around the Mediterranean and beyond. On the other hand, these collections did integrate the key ferry crossings and coasting routes for regions in which the nature of the terrain made taking to water the only sensible option. However, with the independent traveller in mind, the focus was on land routes, in which sphere he or she was not dependent on another's schedule and could therefore use an itinerary to make decisions about timing and direction of travel. Nevertheless, in the attempt of the compiler of the *Itinerarium Antonini* to produce balancing provincial and maritime sections, some fragments of Latin versions of, and home-grown Latin equivalents to, the Greek *periploi* survive. These probably had as limited a circulation as their Greek counterparts, which explains why the anonymous compiler had difficulty laying his hands on information for the maritime portion as comprehensive as that he possessed for the terrestrial. Nevertheless, it is striking that the coverage of the *itinerarium maritimum* almost precisely supplements the lacuna in our Greek works (see fig. 9). The fact that the compiler clearly encountered great difficulty in collecting any information of practical utility for points east of Carthage and the Peloponnese may offer further confirmation of Braudel's contention about the relative exclusivity of the two worlds. Whatever the truth of that assertion, it is clear that in terms of units of measurement the high seas remained a Greek preserve, while the Romans were, to some extent, able to bring their terrestrial miles to bear on those routes that closely hugged the shore.

Holy Land Itineraries:
Mapping the Bible in Late Roman Palestine

E. D. Hunt

The record of pilgrim journeys to the Christian Holy Land begins with the surviving text of the *Bordeaux Itinerary*, the account of an anonymous expedition from the western seaboard of the Roman world to the biblical sites of Jerusalem and Palestine.[1] The journey took place in 333, so a mere 21 years after Constantine's profession of Christianity, and only nine years after his defeat of Licinius and unification of the empire behind the banner of his new faith. When the traveller from Bordeaux arrived in Jerusalem, the new Christian basilica which Constantine had ordered to be erected by the site of the rediscovered Holy Sepulchre was still awaiting its formal dedication, which would occur two years later in September 335. Then Christian bishops would gather in Jerusalem, at Constantine's bidding, not only to inaugurate the emperor's new church, but also to open the celebrations to mark the thirtieth anniversary of his accession – a marriage of ecclesiastical and state ceremonial which placed Jerusalem at that moment at the very centre of the Roman world.[2]

In a recent study Jaś Elsner has skilfully exploited the value of the Bordeaux pilgrim's text as first-hand contemporary testimony to this fusion of Christian and imperial worlds, reflected through the shifting

---

[1] See E.D. Hunt, *Holy Land Pilgrimage in the Later Roman Empire AD 312-460* (Oxford 1982), 55-8, 83-5. For text, see the edition of P. Geyer and O. Cuntz in *Itineraria et Alia Geographica* (Corpus Christianorum Series Latina 175, 1965), 1-26.

[2] Eusebius, *Life of Constantine*, IV.43-8; with E.D. Hunt, 'Constantine and Jerusalem', *JEH* 48 (1997), 419ff.

perceptions of space and geography which it illustrates.[3] The traveller documents his (or her?) passage along the main thoroughfares of the Roman empire from Gaul to the eastern Mediterranean in the characteristic manner of the *itinerarium* (closely resembling the pattern of the material in the 'Antonine' Itinerary).[4] We are presented with (in Elsner's phrase) 'a road-map in words': for the most part a bald and unadulterated list of places and distances, including intermediate nightly halts *(mansiones)* and stops for a change of horses *(mutationes)*. The administrative organisation of the contemporary empire unfolds through the pages of the text, as the pilgrim traverses its roads, passes through cities and crosses provincial boundaries *en route* to his destination. In this case, of course, the roads no longer lead to Rome (except as a staging-post on the return journey through Italy), but firstly to Constantinople, where our traveller draws breath before embarking on the eastern section of his journey;[5] and secondly then to Jerusalem, the ultimate objective. The world which confronts us in this text is thus one whose central axis now stretches from Constantine's newly-founded eponymous capital on the Bosphorus (dedicated as recently as 330[6]) to the emergent holy city of Jerusalem, now in the process of supplanting what had been the Hadrianic *colonia* of Aelia Capitolina.[7]

---

[3]   J. Elsner, 'The *Itinerarium Burdigalense*: politics and salvation in the geography of Constantine's empire', *JRS* 90 (2000), 181-95.

[4]   See, most recently, Benet Salway, 'Travel, *itineraria* and *tabellaria*', in C. Adams & R. Laurence (eds), *Travel and Geography in the Roman Empire* (London, 2001), 22-66. For suggestion of female authorship, L. Douglass, 'A new look at the *Itinerarium Burdigalense*', *JECS* 4 (1996), 313-33, at 328ff.

[5]   It is clear from the organisation of the text that the journey is conceived in two distinct parts, with a 'restart' from Constantinople on the leg to Jerusalem: see Salway, op.cit., 36.

[6]   For the date, 11 May 330, see T.D. Barnes, *Constantine and Eusebius* (Cambridge Mass., 1981), 222.

[7]   On the Constantinian transformation of Jerusalem, see Hunt, *Holy Land Pilgrimage*, 6-27; R.L. Wilken, *The Land Called Holy: Palestine in Christian History and Thought* (New Haven and London, 1992), 82-100; Y. Tsafrir, 'Byzantine Jerusalem: the configuration of a Christian city', in L.I. Levine (ed.), *Jerusalem: its sanctity and centrality to Judaism, Christianity and Islam* (1999), 133-50.

Not only is Jerusalem the goal of the pilgrim's journey: it is the hub of a geography which owes nothing to the contemporary secular map of the Roman empire, and everything to the landscape of Judaeo-Christian history derived from the Bible. Elsner has shown this transformation revealed in the text's virtual abandonment of the dry, administrative itinerary format once it – and its traveller – arrive in the Holy Land, to be replaced by a richly descriptive 'guide-book' detailing the location of biblical events from Old and New Testaments. The pilgrim has put aside his Roman road-map in favour of the pages of Scripture, which now define and identify the topography and landscape in which he moves. Only when he sets out on the return journey from Jerusalem does he re-enter the world of the Roman empire, resuming the bare enumeration of places and distances which had marked his outward travels to the borders of Palestine.

Elsner concluded his study by emphasizing the 'otherness' of the Bordeaux pilgrim's Holy Land: a 'different kind of space' which spoke to religious belief and the history of salvation rather than to the political or administrative realities of the fourth-century Roman empire. This paper will seek to borrow this perspective and test it in relation to another early pilgrim narrative, one already much better known and more widely studied than the Bordeaux text. Some fifty years afterwards, another westerner of uncertain origin journeyed to the holy places of Jerusalem and Palestine, and ventured further afield to visit the holy men of the Egyptian desert: Egeria, a lady of insatiable devotion and intrepid traveller, went on to write up an account of her experiences and address it to fellow-believers back home (her 'revered sisters').[8] Her narrative was certainly circulating in the late seventh

---

[8] The most convenient modern edition of the *Itinerarium Egeriae* (with French translation and notes) is that of P. Maraval, *Egérie: Journal de Voyage* (Sources Chrétiennes 296, Paris 1982). John Wilkinson, *Egeria's Travels* (3rd edn. Warminster, 1999), provides a useful introduction and English translation. See also A. Palmer, 'Egeria the Voyager', in Z von Martels (ed.), *Travel Fact and Travel Fiction* (1994), 39-53. For recent thoughts on the dating of Egeria's journey, see E.D. Hunt, 'The date of the *Itinerarium Egeriae*', in M.F. Wiles and E.J. Yarnold (eds), *Studia Patristica* vol. XXXVIII (Leuven 2001), 410-16.

century in north-western Spain, when Egeria was advertised as a model of spiritual endeavour for the monks of the day;[9] but it was not until 1884 that the manuscript of a portion of her text was discovered in a monastic library in Arezzo. The second half of what survives is Egeria's celebrated observation of the round of the church's liturgy in Jerusalem and elsewhere; the first part finds her, *in medias res*, tracing the steps of the children of Israel in the Sinai desert in the course of their exodus from Egypt, to be followed by other biblical excursions out from Jerusalem, and her eventual return to Constantinople, which included a detour from Antioch into northern Mesopotamia, both to visit local monks and to pray at the shrine of St Thomas at Edessa. With the loss of the beginning of her narrative, it is difficult accurately to categorize the literary form of Egeria's text, but its periodic addresses to her '*sorores*' suggest that it was conceived in the manner of an extended and edifying descriptive letter.[10] In a list of the manuscript holdings, however, of a monastery in tenth-century Spain Egeria's work had already acquired the label of an *itinerarium*, and it was similarly described later in library catalogues at the abbey of St Martial at Limoges.[11] Modern editions of Egeria have tended to favour this classification of her text.[12]

As the compiler of an 'itinerary', even if one incorporated into a fuller narrative structure, Egeria invites comparison with her predecessor from Bordeaux. Her text displays many similar features. She shares, for example, its 'taxonomy of stopping',[13] assiduously punctuating the record of her movements with mentions of nightly halts at *mansiones*,

[9]   See the 'Letter of Valerius', edited by Manuel C. Díaz y Díaz as appendix to Maraval's edition of *It.Eg.* (pp. 323ff.), with English translation in Wilkinson, 200-4.

[10] For discussion of possible audience for Egeria's 'open letter', see H. Sivan, 'Holy Land pilgrimage and western audiences: some reflections on Egeria and her circle', *CQ* 38 (1988), 528-35.

[11] See A. Wilmart, 'L'*Itinerarium Eucheriae*', *Rev. Bénédictine* 25 (1908), 458-67, at 461-3.

[12] So, for example, the standard work of Aet. Franceschini and R. Weber, in *Itineraria et Alia Geographica* (n.1 above), 29-90. The first editor of the Arezzo manuscript, G.F. Gamurrini, had adopted the title 'peregrinatio'.

[13] Elsner, p. 187.

and measuring distances by the number of such stops: so Mt Sinai is '22 *mansiones*' distant from Jerusalem,[14] Jerusalem to Carneas is '8 *mansiones*' (13.2), and Edessa is at the '25th *mansio*' from Jerusalem (17.2). When enquiring of the local bishop at Carrhae for the whereabouts of Abraham's Ur of the Chaldees, Egeria was told that it was no longer accessible to Romans as it now lay within Persian territory, at a distance of ten *mansiones*: 'from here as far as Nisibis there are five *mansiones*, and then another five as far as Ur.'[15] Such alertness to the presence of Roman boundaries is also particularly reminiscent of the Bordeaux document, which regularly recorded the crossing of regional and provincial borders *en route* from Italy through the Balkans and across Asia Minor and Syria.[16] Egeria too was meticulous in noting the crossing of provincial boundaries: on leaving the territory of Palestine, for example, to enter the Egyptian province of Augustamnica, and re-entering Palestine on her return;[17] similarly the two provincial border crossings which were involved in the journey from Antioch to Edessa, that between Coele-Syria and Augusta Euphratensis (where Egeria stayed in the metropolis, Hierapolis), and the ship-board crossing of the Euphrates which was the boundary with the territory of Mesopotamia (18.1-3). Egeria's return across Asia Minor from Antioch to Constantinople was also carefully demarcated by borders, places and distances. From Tarsus, the metropolis of Cilicia, she made a diversion along the coast to visit the shrine of St Thecla at Seleucia (Silifke), which involved a night in the city of Pompeiopolis, crossing the boundary into Isauria, and a second halt at Corycus before arriving at

---

[14] Pet. Diac. *Liber de locis sanctis*, Y4 (ed. R. Weber, *Itineraria et Alia Geographica* [see above], 93-103). This twelfth-century gazetteer of the Holy Land, derived in large part from Egeria, is used by editors to reconstruct the lost portion of her text (see also Maraval, pp. 104-5; Wilkinson, p. 101).

[15] 20.12: making 363, the year of Jovian's surrender of Nisibis and surrounding territory to the Persians, the *terminus post quem* for Egeria's visit to the region.

[16] Elsner, 187-8.

[17] 9.7, cf. Pet. Diac. *loc. cit.* for outward journey. On Augustamnica among the provinces of late Roman Egypt, note R.S. Bagnall, *Egypt in Late Antiquity* (Princeton, 1993), 63-4.

her destination 'on the third day'(23.1)[18]. After returning to Tarsus, and
a three-day break there, she set off on the final leg, spending the first
night at the same *mansio* of Mansucrenae which had afforded hospitality
to the Bordeaux pilgrim:[19] 'thence the next day I climbed Mount
Taurus and travelled the now familiar journey through each of the provinces which I had passed on my way, Cappadocia, Galatia and
Bithynia, until I reached Chalcedon' (23.7; Egeria's narrative, we may
presume, had provided the full itinerary in recounting the outward
journey, as had the Bordeaux traveller before her[20]). From Chalcedon
she crossed the Bosphorus and entered Constantinople.

Egeria's account of her travels between Jerusalem and Constantinople, as of her forays out from Jerusalem, was thus cast (like the Bordeaux itinerary) in the pattern of the administrative geography of the
contemporary Roman empire. The information which her predecessor
had compiled into a bare catalogue of places and distances was
embedded by Egeria into a fuller narrative, the 'road-map in words'
functioning as a framework in her case for a continuous prose description of her movements through Asia Minor. For her, just as for the
Bordeaux traveller, Jerusalem and Constantinople were the twin
centres of gravity. Although we are hampered in not having the earlier
part of her account which had described her arrival in Jerusalem three
years previously and her initial reaction to its holy places, it is clear
enough from the surviving chapters on the cycle of worship that the
holy city was central to Egeria's Christian geography, a perception
which she was eager to share with her sisters in the west who would
'want to know' about the daily pattern of services in Jerusalem (24.1). It
was, moreover, her arrival and departure from Jerusalem specifically
which defined for Egeria the limits of her stay in the Holy Land.[21] And

---

[18] On this shrine of Thecla, see now S.J. Davis, *The Cult of St Thecla: a tradition of women's piety in late antiquity* (Oxford, 2001), ch. 2.

[19] Cf. *It. Burd.* 579, 2. In the meantime the place ('the last station in Cilicia as
you come from here, situated at the foot of Mount Taurus') had entered
history as the location of Constantius II's death in November 361: Amm.
Marc. 21.15.2.

[20] *It. Burd.* 571, 9-580, recording 33 *mansiones* between Chalcedon and Tarsus.

[21] 'Some time after that, since it was already three full years since my arrival

it was Constantinople which provided the pivotal point of her journey there and back. On returning to Constantine's city she brought a note of finality to her journey by visiting its churches and martyr-shrines to give thanks to God for the blessings of her pilgrimage; and it was from Constantinople in this same mood of recollection and grateful completion of her objective that she committed to writing the narrative which has come down to us.[22] The Bordeaux traveller had already signalled Constantinople as the chief port-of-call from west to east, and a new point of departure for the onward journey across the eastern empire to Jerusalem. But whereas the earlier document conceived the city as foremost in the secular and administrative geography of the Roman empire,[23] for Egeria it was a good deal more than this. Her Constantinople was akin to Jerusalem at the hub of a Christian world, a holy place with Christian shrines providing a fitting environment to round off her devotions and recall her pilgrimage for her like-minded correspondents. The image of Egeria on her knees amid the churches of Constantinople effectively unites what in Elsner's analysis of the Bordeaux itinerary had been juxtaposed as two separate worlds and two distinct 'kinds of space'. The two worlds are here fused and intertwined. While in physical terms separated from Jerusalem by a land journey which traversed one of the principal routes of the Roman empire across provincial boundaries and passing through an established

in Jerusalem, and I had seen all the places which were the object of my pilgrimage, I felt that the time had come to return in God's name to my own country' (17.1, transl. Wilkinson).

[22] 'Next day I crossed the sea and reached Constantinople, giving thanks to Christ our God for seeing fit, through no deserving of mine, to grant me the desire to go on this journey, and the strength to visit everything I wanted and now to return again to Constantinople. And in all the churches at Constantinople, in the tombs of the apostles, and at many martyria, I never ceased to give thanks to Jesus our God for his grace in showing such mercy. So, loving ladies, light of my heart, this is where I am writing to you' (23.8-10, transl. Wilkinson).

[23] Cf. Salway (n. 4 above), p. 36, interpreting the Jerusalem venture as an addition to some kind of 'official' journey to Constantinople.

network of cities and *mansiones*, Egeria's Constantinople shared a
'spiritual' unity with Jerusalem within the totality of a Christian geography – and history: Jerusalem pre-eminently owed its holiness to its
Judaeo-Christian past, and Constantinople too had now come to
acquire a Christian heritage of apostles and martyrs, at whose shrines
Egeria worshipped.[24]

The fact is that Egeria's narrative, at least what survives of it, will
not permit the kind of easy disentanglement, part secular itinerary, part
sacred 'Baedeker', which the Bordeaux text invites by its more obvious
bipartite form and structure. Her travels, as she describes them, displayed both characteristics simultaneously. It is also the case that her
account offers a far greater sense of *engagement* in a journey which is at
one and the same time both practical itinerary and spiritual pilgrimage.
The Bordeaux document is a markedly more *detached* composition, not
only in its administrative lists of places and distances (where the only
obvious hint of a real journey in progress comes with the formal
announcement, in the first person plural, of the exact dates – by consular year – of the departure from and return to Constantinople),[25] but
even in its more expansive Holy Land core, which is couched almost
entirely as an impersonal gazetteer of locations accurately labelled by
their scriptural references. Elsner's talk of the 'otherness' of the journey through Palestine is encouraged by this sense of distancing and
detachment from its objectives. Egeria's narrative, by contrast, provides a record intensely *involved* in its journey, making regular use of the
first person, and by its direct address to the '*sorores*' far away in the
west, engaging them too in the progress of the travels and the locations
being described. The actual itinerary and the biblical journey confront-
ing the places of scripture appear to have merged into a single experience.

---

[24] On Constantinople's acquisition of a Christian past through the import of
apostles' relics, see H. Delehaye, *Les Origines du Culte des Martyrs* (Subsidia
Hagiographica 20, 2nd edn. Brussels 1933), 55-7; C. Mango, 'Constantine's Mausoleum and the Translation of Relics', *Byz. Zeitschr.* 83 (1990), 51-
61, at pp. 59-60, with his addendum, *ibid.* p. 434.

[25] *It. Burd.* 571, 6-8: 30 May–26 December 333.

Nor was it solely the 'sisters' addressed who were drawn into Egeria's travelling: there were other people with her, and many besides encountered on the way. Apart from the one anonymous plural to denote the beginning and end of the expedition, the Bordeaux text afforded no indication of travelling companions, nor of hosts and guides at places visited – its journey was abstracted, disembodied from any real experience of travel.[26] Egeria too, to be fair, has nothing to say of her immediate circle of fellow-travellers (except, of course, that her addressees are conceived of as sharing the progress of her journey), but she is enthusiastically vocal about the company she found in and around the holy places. Hers is a crowded lansdcape, populated chiefly by the monks and their clergy who greeted her travelling-party at their ports-of-call, provided them with hospitality, pointed them to the scriptural locations which were the object of the enterprise, conducted the obligatory acts of worship at the sites, and when all was seen and done accompanied them on their way. These monks were central to the formulation of Egeria's pilgrimage and the definition of its scriptural terrain, at the heart of this simultaneous amalgam of contemporary actuality and biblical past so characteristic of her movements. They had a foot in both worlds, ideally placed to serve as intermediaries between the two 'different kinds of space' – at once providing the mechanisms to facilitate the present itinerary, places to stay and escorts along the way, and unlocking access to the sacred landscape of the past by showing her the places and expounding their scriptural history. Egeria's monks inhabit both the late fourth-century of the eastern Roman empire and also the land of the Bible, in which context they live on in her eyes as the successors of patriarchs and prophets of old. The latter peopled Egeria's reading of her Old Testament, while the monks functioned as the *dramatis personae* of these biblical events as she relived them in the Holy Land of her day.[27]

---

[26] On the impression of 'social emptiness' conveyed by the Bordeaux traveller, cf. B. Leyerle, 'Landscape as Cartography in Early Christian Pilgrimage Narratives', *Journ. Amer. Acad. Rel.* 64 (1996), 119-43, at p. 126.

[27] Cf. Leyerle, 128-9, on Egeria's 'level of emotional investment' in her travels; with E.D. Hunt, 'The Itinerary of Egeria: reliving the Bible in fourth-century Palestine', in R.N. Swanson (ed.), *The Holy Land, Holy*

A rather more specific illustration of the kind of spatial and tem-
poral amalgam which runs through Egeria's narrative can be derived
from the chapters (6-9) recounting her return to Jerusalem from the
holy mountain of Sinai, where we first discover her in the surviving
portion of the text. Egeria would retrace her steps along the eastern
shore of the Gulf of Suez to Clysma (modern Suez), then divert north-
westwards (for reasons which will become apparent)[28] eventually to
join the main route from upper Egypt via the eastern arm of the Nile
delta to Pelusium, and on round the coast to Palestine and Jerusalem.
As already noted above, this is a journey marked out according to the
conventions of a contemporary itinerary and the administrative organisation of the Roman empire. It is measured in Roman miles and over-
night *mansiones*; it carefully demarcates the crossing of provincial boundaries between Egypt and Palestine; and it notes the point at which
Egeria's route met up with the 'public road' from the Thebaid to Pelusium.[29] It was at this junction that her party regained safety, leaving behind the military escort which, she reports, had had to accompany
them, in the interests of *disciplina romana*, for the four stages through
the desert from Suez (7.2, 9.3); this section of her journey, labelled a
'danger zone' ('loca suspecta'), brought Egeria into districts exposed to
marauding raids from Saracen tribesmen, and Suez itself and other
places along her way were protected by fortified posts ('castra').[30] No

Lands, and Christian History (= *Studies in Church History*, vol. 36), (Wood-
bridge, 2000), 34-54, at 46ff., and H.S. Sivan, 'Pilgrimage, monasticism
and the emergence of Christian Palestine', in R. Ousterhout (ed.), *The Blessings of Pilgrimage* (Urbana, 1990), 54-65. For pilgrims 'visualising' the biblical past in the persons of contemporary monks, see now G. Frank, *The
Memory of the Eyes: Pilgrims to Living Saints in Late Antiquity* (Berkeley, 2000).

[28]   See below pp. 107-108.

[29]   9.3 ('ager publicum'); Wilkinson aptly translates 'the *state highway* from the
       Thebaid to Pelusium'.

[30]   Egeria's experience of the area's insecurity is paralleled by a (problemati-
       cal) Sinai martyr tradition set against the background of late fourth-century
       Saracen raids: see I. Shahîd, *Byzantium and the Arabs in the Fourth Century*
       (Washington, 1984), 297-319; Z. Rubin, 'Sinai in the *Itinerarium Egeriae*', in
       Atti del Convegno Internazionale sulla Peregrinatio Egeriae (Arezzo, 1990), 177-

doubt, then, that this was a trip being undertaken in pressing contemporary conditions at the remote edges of the Roman empire. Other, less threatening aspects of the present-day world impressed themselves on Egeria's perceptions: the ships from 'India' at anchor in the harbour at Suez,[31] or the markers in the sand which enabled the local bedouin to navigate the way with their camels (6.2). Natural features of the contemporary landscape also framed the depiction of her journeying: the waters lapping round the feet of their horses as they followed the seashore (6.1), or the rich fertility of the banks of the Nile '... vineyards, orchards, well-kept fields and magnificent gardens. All the way the road followed the banks of the Nile. ... I think I have never seen a more beautiful landscape ...' (9.4). By now Egeria was back on the main road to Pelusium and the route to Palestine and her base at Jerusalem: 'I returned to Aelia, that is to say Jerusalem' (9.7). Only here, at least in what survives of her narrative, does Egeria admit the official Roman name of Jerusalem, Aelia Capitolina, which it had carried since the foundation of the Hadrianic *colonia* and would continue to do so into Byzantine times.[32] It was a fittingly Roman terminus for an itinerary which had brought her along the 'public road' from Egypt into Palestine, via the ten *mansiones* which separated Pelusium from Jerusalem.[33]

But Aelia was also the biblical Jerusalem; and the fertile farms which had attracted Egeria's attention from the road along the Nile 'had once been the estates of the children of Israel' (9.4). Indeed the only reason why Egeria returned the way she did from Suez (rather than travel directly north to Pelusium) was 'so that I might see all the places where the children of Israel had been on their way from Ramesses to the Red

---

91.

[31] Pet. Diac. *Liber de locis sanctis*, Y6 (cf. n. 14 above). She is mistaken in claiming that Clysma (Suez) was the sole port in Roman territory to receive vessels from India; according to Pliny, *Nat. Hist.* VI. 103, the Red Sea harbour of Berenice was the starting-point for the Indian trade.

[32] On the survival of the name 'Aelia', see Hunt, *Holy Land Pilgrimage*, p. 149.

[33] Cf. n. 14 above, for distances from Jerusalem to Sinai and from Pelusium to Sinai.

Sea' (7.1). Her present-day itinerary was also her scriptural pilgrimage; and those fertile lands beside the Nile were equally the biblical 'land of Goshen', where Jacob and his sons had first settled when they arrived in Egypt, and whence the exodus began. Egeria's narrative can be seen simultaneously to move through the Egyptian landscape of her own day and to plot a course which studiously replicates the early books of the Old Testament.[34] Thus, for example, on returning from Sinai to Suez,

> ... we left the mountains at the same point where we had entered them, and turned to go along beside the sea; this is just what the children of Israel did, rejoining the Red Sea after coming back here from Sinai, the mount of God, to the point where we emerged from the mountains. From this point we "went our way" back by the road by which we had come, and it was from the same point that the children of Israel "went their way" as we are told in the books of Moses.   (6.3, transl. Wilkinson)

Not only does Egeria meticulously reproduce the biblical wanderings in her own movements – interchanging the first and third person in her narrative – but improves on them to the extent of equipping the Israelites with identifiable locations and a degree of topographical precision which she could not have found in her Bible (where there is a profusion of place-names, and mention of various wildernesses and mountains, but nothing which amounts to a 'map' of the route).[35] The placing of all the scriptural sites was surely the work of her monastic guides, eager to feed her hunger for a tangible biblical topography by translating the Israelites' movements on to the surrounding landscape.[36] Monks were certainly leading Egeria and her company when, instead of proceeding directly north from Suez to the coast at Pelusi-

---

[34] Cf. Leyerle, p. 128 'Egeria's travel account illustrates the creation of the holy land as a map of scriptural events'.

[35] The account of the exodus from Egypt begins at *Exodus* 12.37; Sinai is reached at *Exodus* 19.1, and the journey thence is resumed at *Numbers* 10.12. *Numbers* 33 provides a summary 'itinerary'.

[36] For the monks' 'manipulation of landscape', cf. Sivan (n. 27 above), p. 55.

um, she diverted to visit the 'land of Goshen', and thus retrace in reverse the biblical exodus to the Red Sea:

> all the way I kept asking to see the different places mentioned in the Bible,
> and they were all pointed out to me by the holy men, the clergy and monks
> with us. Some of the places were to the right and others to the left of our
> route, some a long way off and others close by. So, as far as I can see,
> loving sisters, believe me that the children of Israel walked in such a way
> that as far as they went to the right so they came back to the left, and as
> far as they moved forwards, so they moved back again ...
>
> (7.2-3, adapted from Wilkinson)

Egeria here typically seeks to involve her far-off 'sisters' as fellow-
travellers on these circuitous biblical peregrinations, but the frustrations of providing the book of Exodus with a visible geography in the
Egypt of the late fourth century A.D. tested even her devotional
curiosity. When she eventually reached the place identified for her as
Ramesses, the starting-point of the biblical exodus, she found nothing
but a vast extent of ruins, two stone statues and an ancient sycamore
tree. The local bishop told her that the statues were of Moses and
Aaron, that the sycamore tree had been planted by the patriarchs, and
that the ruins were the result of Pharaoh's drastic reprisals after learning of the escape of the Israelites (8.1-5). In the Bible Ramesses is only
a name; but in the interests of reinforcing its location as part of a
visible biblical terrain, of creating a biblical geography, apocryphal
stories were needed to account for the appearance of the site in
Egeria's day.[37]

It would be easy to conclude from this material that Egeria had
abandoned her real world for a fantasy journey in company with Moses
and his people. But that would be to ignore the continuing 'reality' of
Egeria's experience of moving around this corner of the Roman
empire as it was in her day. At the same time as monks were answering
to her biblical appetite, Roman soldiers were protecting her passage
through dangerous reaches of the desert: indeed at one point her text

---

[37] On the location of 'Ramesses', see Maraval, p. 159 n.2; Wilkinson, p. 117
n.3.

may indicate that soldiers and monks together manned the fortified
mansiones which marked the route.[38] She was alive, too, to the contrast
presented by the sight of the places through which she now passed
with the appearance of their biblical forbears: not just that present-day
security needs had transformed them into military forts, but also, for
example, in the case of the place where Joseph had met his father
Jacob on his arrival in Egypt, what was identified as a 'city' in her text
of Genesis is now, she says, 'a village ... what we call a *vicus*.'[39] At the
end of her desert journey from Suez Egeria stayed in the 'city of
Arabia' (7.9, cf. 7.1): the name was drawn from her Bible, where the
Septuagint translators had glossed the 'land of Goshen' as the 'land of
Arabia'; but it was not just a long obsolete biblical label, for the name
'Arabia' had been part of the administrative map of Ptolemaic Egypt
and would continue to designate this district throughout the Roman
period.[40]

When, therefore, Egeria described her arrival 'at the city which is
called Arabia, which city is in the land of Goshen', she was charting
movements which belonged simultaneously in her own times and in
those of the Exodus, and which equally embraced two different kinds
of space. Hers was a journey comprised of two overlapping and con-
current itineraries, one recognisably set in the contemporary map of
the Roman empire, the other extrapolated from the pages of the Bible.
Whereas for the Bordeaux pilgrim the borders of Palestine had demarcated the one from the other, in Egeria's case the two worlds never
ceased to intersect, no matter what road she travelled.

[38] 7.2 'ut cata mansionses *monasteria* sint cum militibus et prepositis', if 'monasteria' is to be understood in its normal monastic sense: cf. Maraval, p.
154 n.1.
[39] 7.7: Egeria has a Latin transcription ('Heroum civitas') of the Greek name
found in the Septuagint translation of *Genesis* 46.28. On the text of the
Bible used by Egeria, still valuable is J. Ziegler, 'Die Peregrinatio Aetheriae
und die hl. Schrift', *Biblica* 12 (1931), 162-98.
[40] Egeria was following the Septuagint version of *Genesis* 45.10, 46.34, 47.6,
which identified Goshen with the Ptolemaic district of 'Arabia'. For the
persistence of the name into Byzantine times, see Maraval, p. 158 n.1.

The *Tabula Peutingeriana*

Cartography and Taste in Peutinger's Roman Map[*]

Richard Talbert

When colleagues ask what is now engaging my attention after the completion of the *Barrington Atlas of the Greek and Roman World* (Princeton and Oxford, 2000), and I mention Peutinger's Roman map,[1] it is clear that they are puzzled. They regard the map as a thoroughly studied document from which little more is likely to be learned. Their impression is understandable, but in fact misplaced. Rather, the Peutinger map belongs in that deceptive category of ancient texts or monuments so familiar to everyone in our field that a satisfactory edition or presentation is generally assumed to exist, when really there is none. To be sure, in this instance there has been one outstanding attempt, a monumental volume containing much of lasting value, but old now and inevitably long overdue for replacement. This massive *Itineraria Romana* by Konrad Miller (1844-1933) was published in 1916 of all tragic years, in Stuttgart, and reflects work done intermittently as far back as the 1880s, including a revision of the standard engraving of the map by Franz Christoph von Scheyb (1753). Even after the publication of full-size photographs of the entire map in 1888 (in mono-

---

[*] This is a revised and somewhat expanded version of the paper read in Glasgow in March 2001. I appreciate the insights of all those who contributed to the discussion there, and subsequently on other occasions in Calgary, Saskatoon, Providence RI, and Rome. I also acknowledge with deep thanks generous support for this ongoing research from the American Council of Learned Societies, the J.S. Guggenheim Foundation, and the National Humanities Center.

[1] I fully support O.A.W. Dilke's call to abandon the traditional name of 'Peutinger Table' or 'Tabula Peutingeriana', "to avoid any misconception that the original image was somehow carved on a table or was like a statistical table" (238 n. 25 in J.B. Harley and D. Woodward [eds.], *The History of Cartography*, vol. 1, Chicago, 1987).

chrome), Miller continued to rely upon, and to reproduce, his own revised engraving. In the longer term, reliance upon color photographs would naturally have been still more desirable for study, as soon as their publication became practical. It was not until 1976, however, that color photographs of the Peutinger map appeared.[2]

Miller was neither a trained classical scholar, nor even a professional academic. Instead, it was newfound enthusiasm for Roman archaeology that attracted him to the map.[3] Thus, in line with the choice of title, his *Itineraria Romana* aims primarily to test the accuracy of the routes and distances shown on the map against surviving material or documentary testimony for conditions on the ground. For ease of presentation, he divides up the map in accordance with the boundaries of the Roman empire's fourth-century administrative dioceses, and then follows routes ('Strecken') within each diocese, place by place. It must be appreciated, however, that often the courses determined for individual routes are purely of his own devising, and that neither names nor boundaries of dioceses appear on the map. In the same prescriptive vein, Miller readily rewrites lettering and redraws linework to eliminate what he perceives to be error or confusion.[4]

---

[2] See the Appendix below for an overview of reproductions of the map since 1753.

[3] Note the two memoirs by his grand-niece, Gertrud Husslein – valuable not least for reflecting his astonishing energy, and the breadth and depth of his talents and interests – in H. Gaube (ed.), *Konrad Miller, Mappae Arabicae*, *TAVO* Beihefte B65, Wiesbaden, 1986, IX-XIII, and more fully in *Orbis Terrarum* 1 [1995] 213-33 with Tafeln 13-17. In the first memoir, she slips in stating (XI) that Miller's imaginative reconstruction of the Peutinger map's missing lefthand parchment originally appeared as early as 1888 (see Appendix below). Husslein was responsible for one of the reprintings of Miller's *Itineraria Romana* (Bregenz, 1988).

[4] This impatient, opinionated approach was perhaps characteristic. Compare the observation by S.D. Westrem, *The Hereford Map: a Transcription and Translation of the Legends with Commentary* (Turnhout, 2001): "Miller, by his own admission, never saw the Hereford Map. His published facsimile [1896], which is 3/7 the size of the map itself, includes altered text that corresponds to his readings (incorrect, and apparently derived from what

Since 1916, scholars with an interest in a specific route or region have consistently paid due attention to the Peutinger map,[5] but there has been no comprehensive reappraisal. The only attempt I am aware of is one by Otto Cuntz (1858-1932), but it was evidently abandoned after his death.[6] During the past half-century in particular, the dif-

he thought a reading ought to be); in some cases his readings and facsimile clearly disagree" (xxvi n. 35). Miller did at least examine the Peutinger map himself.

[5] In *L'Année Philologique*, under 'Auteurs et textes', search such entries as 'Tabula Peutingeriana' (or vice versa) and 'Itineraria et geographica'. Note also, for example, the extensive bibliography appended to M. Calzolari, "Gli itinerari della tarda antichità e il nodo stradale di Aquileia", pp. 18-41 in S. Blason Scarel (ed.), *Cammina, Cammina... Dalla Via dell' Ambra alla Via della Fede* (Aquileia, 2000).

[6] In the brief Praefatio to his *Itineraria Romana* I (Leipzig, 1929), Cuntz records that the original intention was for the Roman itineraries to be edited jointly by Wilhelm Kubitschek (1858-1936) and himself. But once Kubitschek had become otherwise preoccupied, Cuntz determined to press ahead alone, and following this first volume of the pair he next means to issue the second containing "tabulae Peutingerianae itinera, geographum Ravennatem, itineraria minora". However, when a second volume did appear, in 1940, the sole editor, Joseph Schnetz (1873-1952), explains at the beginning of the Praefatio that Cuntz had died in December 1932, leaving "nihil nisi quae ad editionem Tabulae Peutingerianae praeparaverat". Schnetz, because of his prior work on the Ravenna Geographer, preferred to limit the second volume to this text and that of Guido, *Geographica*, with an additional third one to follow; it never has. The second volume even lacked an index until this was added by M. Zumschlinge, when both volumes were reissued with some more recent bibliography (in vol. 1, by G. Wirth) in 1990. From his own allusion (1929, p. VII), the impression must be that Cuntz's approach to the Peutinger map would have matched Miller's, with close attention to names and distance figures, and variants in the recording of both. Kubitschek was not slow to find much fault with Miller's work (note the severe reviews in *Göttingische gelehrte Anzeigen* 179 [1917] 1-117 and *Zeitschrift für die deutsch-österreichischen Gymnasien* 68 [1917/18] 740-54 and 865-93); even so, it has proved indispensable and has yet to be replaced.

ficulties of replicating Miller's achievement have become quite over-whelming, and they only increase annually with the continuing high level of activity in archaeology and epigraphy. Today, without a reliable and reasonably up-to-date synthesis of routes to serve as foundation, even a team of scholars would be hard-pressed to cover the entire map in the way that Miller did single-handed. Fortunately, since 2000 the *Barrington Atlas of the Greek and Roman World* and its accompanying *Map-by-Map Directory* have provided such a foundation. Among much else, between them they do represent, and document, current knowledge of principal routes, so that to make a comparison with the Peutinger map in this regard at long last becomes practicable.

Meantime, other developments of importance have occurred. The traditional, narrow preoccupation with whether an ancient historical or geographical text, or map, is 'accurate' has been overtaken by a broader concern to approach it on its own terms, and to appreciate what it reflects of the author's purpose and taste, regardless of its 'accuracy' from a modern perspective.[7] More specifically, during the past fifteen years there has arisen a debate (still ongoing) about ancient map-consciousness, and in particular about the extent to which Romans made maps and used them. As a remarkable example of Roman map-making the Peutinger map has no match, and could thus fairly be expected to play a key role in the discussion. In the event, however, that has not been the case. Not only are the map's sheer size and rich detail forbidding, but there is also simply no study which has sought to evaluate it as a piece of creative cartography. Moreover, the mere fact that it is a map has inclined revisionist participants in the debate

---

[7] Note, for example, D. Wood, *The Power of Maps* (New York, 1992); C.D.K. Yee, "A reaction to the reaction against scientism: on the power and limits of the textual analogy for maps," pp. 203-22 in D. Woodward, C. Delano-Smith and C.D.K. Yee, *Plantejaments I Objectius d' una Història Universal de la Cartografia/Approaches and Challenges in a Worldwide History of Cartography* (Barcelona, 2001); and the pointers offered by D.G. Burnett, *Masters of All They Surveyed: Exploration, Geography, and a British El Dorado* (Chicago, 2000), 5-7.

(myself among them)[8] to focus attention elsewhere, as part of their effort to rethink the established, modernizing assumption that among Romans maps were made and used much as they are today. It is natural enough, therefore, for the fullest contribution to the debate – Kai Brodersen's invaluable 1995 monograph *Terra Cognita*[9] – to devote barely two pages (186-87) to the Peutinger map, on the grounds that it offers no more than a diagrammatic representation of information already available in purely written lists, above all in the so-called *Antonine Itinerary*.[10] Both in his monograph, and elsewhere more recently, Brodersen characterizes the Peutinger map as a "route diagram" in a style matching that of the modern London Tube map, or a European communications outline map.[11] My own current thinking, by contrast, is that this view seriously undervalues the Peutinger map from a cartographic perspective. I would suggest that whoever created it was no newcomer to mapmaking, but must have had extensive prior knowledge and experience of such work; no less can the intended users or recipients have been unfamiliar with maps.

* * * * * *

We should not delay further, however, in turning to the Peutinger map itself – held by the National Library in Vienna, Austria – a copy made on parchment around A.D. 1200 of a Roman original of inde-

---

[8] See, for example, my review of O.A.W. Dilke, *Greek and Roman Maps*, in *JRS* 77 (1987) 210-12.

[9] K.Brodersen, *Terra Cognita. Studien zur römischen Raumerfassung, Spudasmata* 59, Hildesheim, 1995 (²2003).

[10] On this work note now the overview (esp. 39-43) by B. Salway, "Travel, *itineraria* and *tabellaria*," pp. 22-66 in C. Adams and R. Laurence (eds.), *Travel and Geography in the Roman Empire* (London and New York, 2001).

[11] *Terra Cognita*, 64; fig. 2.4 and p. 19 in K. Brodersen, "The presentation of geographical knowledge for travel and transport in the Roman world: *itineraria non tantum adnotata sed etiam picta*," pp. 7-21 in Adams and Laurence 2001 (n. 10 above).

terminate date, although the fourth century seems most likely.[12] From here on, simply for convenience, I refer to the mapmaker as a male in the singular, while readily acknowledging that 'he' could just as well have been a team,[13] and not necessarily an all-male one. I also leave open the unanswerable question of whether it was the mapmaker himself who determined the map's basic design features, or whether these were prescribed by a prospective user who commissioned the work. Either way, we need to appreciate that three bold, interlocking decisions were taken at the outset, which together pose formidable challenges for the mapmaker. They are, first, the map's height; second, its coverage; and third, the placement of Rome. I comment on each in turn.

First, the height is not to exceed about 30 or 31 cm, with an extra 2 or 3 to allow for margins as a frame top and bottom (cf. fig. 13). Such a modest choice creates a notably compact and portable object, and also permits the map to be laid out on a series of mass-produced, standard-size papyrus sheets, which just need to be pasted together left and right to form a roll of whatever length is wanted (assuming that the map either was a papyrus roll originally, or was designed to resemble one). This was the regular format for a text, and it would appear that papyrus sheets were typically never made much taller.[14]

---

[12] For summary discussion of the manuscript and its history since its rediscovery early in the sixteenth century, see the excellent *Kommentar* volume issued by E. Weber to accompany his color reproduction (Graz, 1976; and the Appendix below).

[13] Note that the verses attached to a (lost) world map revised and copied for Theodosius II in 435 specifically refer to lettering as the contribution of one worker, landscape that of another ("... dum scribit pingit et alter"): *GLM*, pp. 19-20, with translation by Dilke 1987 (n. 1 above), 259.

[14] The height of a roll 27.3 cm tall is described by P.J. Parsons as being "at the upper end of the range" (153): see his "Rhetorical handbook," pp. 153-65 in T. Gagos and R.S. Bagnall (eds.), *Essays and Texts in Honor of J. David Thomas, American Studies in Papyrology* 42. 2001. Prof. Gagos informs me that he is not aware of any papyrus sheet taller than approximately 40 cm.

For a map with the coverage expected of this one, however, the standard text format seems far from ideal, and why it was made the choice is matter for speculation. Taller maps as such were by no means unknown,[15] and some must have been drawn on papyrus. In all likelihood, the world-map for which Ptolemy offers specifications in his *Geography* would need to be at least one metre high by two broad.[16] By definition, the production of such a tall map on papyrus would call for standard-size sheets to be pasted together horizontally as well as vertically, and the stylus would then have to negotiate more sheet-joins. Even so, we might expect any anxiety over such minor obstacles to be outweighed by the greater scope gained for layout; but in the case of the Peutinger map that was evidently not a decisive consideration.

If its maker somehow or other had the height of the map imposed upon him, he may well have felt yet further challenged when he learned (second) the required coverage. Eastwards, we know that this extends to the Indian sub-continent and Sri Lanka. Westwards, the limit of coverage remains indeterminable because that end is lost (cf. fig. 14). At a minimum, however, there must be a strong likelihood that England and Wales were included (only the south-east survives), and that coverage of North Africa and mainland Europe continued to the Atlantic Ocean (including the Iberian peninsula, which is lost almost in its entirety). The map as it survives runs to 11 pieces of parchment, each about 60 cm wide, or actually 674 in total; they comprised a single seamless roll until 1863, when the pieces were separated for better preservation.[17] Miller was bold enough to attempt a reconstruction of

[15] For example, the largest (B) of the three stone cadasters at Orange must have measured (in metres) at least 7 x 5.5 tall, and Rome's Marble Plan (*Forma Urbis*) approximately 18.3 x 13: see Dilke 1987 (n. 1 above), 223, 226.

[16] Calculation by J.L. Berggren and A. Jones, *Ptolemy's* Geography: *an Annotated Translation of the Theoretical Chapters*, Princeton and Oxford, 2000, 47. Strabo (2.5.10) gives instructions for drawing a map that is to be at least seven feet in length.

[17] The division into 11 parchment pieces reflects no more than convenience for the copyist; it does not offer any clue to how the mapmaker himself proceeded in this respect. Without question, however, the map was

the lost western end, but he proved strangely cautious in reckoning that only a single further piece of parchment would suffice;[18] this would give an overall length of about 735 cm.

I certainly echo the doubts voiced about whether the mapmaker would have confined himself to using only one parchment to represent all the land area likely to be missing,[19] especially if the coverage extended beyond the Roman empire here in the West, as we see that it did in the East. At the western end, Scotland, Ireland, Madeira and the Canaries could all have been included. Moreover, conceivably there was also some combination of captions, lists and a dedication placed adjacent to the map, but still forming part of the design. We may recall that Ptolemy, for his main map, supplies a caption that amounts to three full pages of a recent English translation.[20] It is natural to think that the Peutinger map was produced for one or more patrons, or at their request, so that a dedication would by no means be a surprise. Equally, lists or a table of total distances between main settlements could be placed adjacent to the map; such total figures are a typical, and obviously useful, component of written itineraries (including the *Stadiasmus Maris Magni*),[21] but are absent from this map. Altogether I think there is ample cause to reckon that two, or even three, parch-

---

designed to be read as a single, seamless whole, regardless of how it was produced or copied.

[18] Taf. 5 in his *Mappaemundi: die ältesten Weltkarten*, Heft 6 (Stuttgart, 1898). A clear illustration of Miller's undue caution is to be found in his bunching of the capitals AQU here, to link up with ITANIA spread across 1B1-1B5. It is uncharacteristic of the mapmaker to lay out a region-name of this type with notable variations in the spacing between each of its letters. We can fairly assume that the spacing of the lost letters AQU would correspond more closely to the layout of the remainder of the name on parchment 1 than to Miller's reconstruction.

[19] See, for example, Weber, *Kommentar* (n. 12 above), 13.

[20] *Geog.* 7.5.1 (or 2)-16 Nobbe = Berggren and Jones 2000 (n. 16 above), 108-11.

[21] See, for example, the points made by Salway in Adams and Laurence 2001 (n. 10 above), esp. 32-34.

ments have been lost at the western end rather than just one; their restoration would make the overall length 795 cm or even 855 (at 60 cm per parchment).

To both south and north, the map's coverage for the most part matches the furthest recognized land routes. Consequently, in Africa it stops short of the desert except in Egypt; within mainland Europe, the Rhine and Danube rivers serve as northern limits west of Dacia. In short, the map spans the Roman *orbis terrarum*. The mapmaker, however, may have been alternately horrified or intrigued at the prospect of having to compress it all – from Britain to as far south as India – within a frame no taller than about 30 cm. In whatever way he normally visualized or represented this span, it was surely not in such a flattened form; the same doubt might be expressed about the vision of whoever was to acquire the map. The 'normal' vision of both (whatever form it took exactly) is likely to have been a less flattened one, which was now to be adapted to fit a frame of distinctly restrictive height. As to the length that the mapmaker might determine for the map, this would by definition also have to take into account the nature and density of physical and cultural data selected for inclusion; but otherwise he may have been relieved at the prospect of gaining some scope to fix the map's length himself.

Or, maybe, he was offered less scope in this regard than he might have hoped for, because (third) he may well have been told where Rome had to be placed, and (if so) his task would only become still more complicated. Miller's reconstruction (supplementing what survives by no more than a single parchment at the western end) sets Rome at the center of the Mediterranean. However, the most ambitious alternative hypothesis (supplementing what survives by as many as three parchments) is even more attractive in that it sets Rome precisely at the center of the entire map. Either way, it seems appropriate to conclude that the placement of Rome is a very deliberate one,[22] and

---

[22] It no doubt contributes in turn to the prominence accorded to Italy, which benefits from exceptionally generous coverage in relation to its land area (about three and a half parchment-widths, from the far right of parchment 2 well into parchment 6).

a key consideration in settling the layout of the map as a whole.[23]

Next, the mapmaker's choices of physical and cultural data for inclusion should be briefly noted. The red linework for routes stands out clearly, with the names of over 2,700 settlements or stations along the way, and a figure for the length of each stage. In principle, written sources alone, like the *Antonine Itinerary* and 'signposts' at major intersections, could supply all this data.[24] Even so, that does not make it appropriate to regard the Peutinger map as merely a diagrammatic representation of routes and their associated placenames and distances. This is simply Miller's choice of perspective that, under his influence, has been adhered to universally ever since, to the point where (as noted above) Brodersen likens the map to modern schematic ones such as the London Tube diagram. But that type of map derives much of its success and popularity from the deliberate exclusion of as many 'irrelevant' or 'extraneous' features as possible;[25] the Peutinger map, by contrast, is nowhere near so focused. Rather, the routes are set within a physical representation of the main land masses, marked out by their shorelines and manipulated to fit the most elongated frame imaginable. This manipulation by the mapmaker merits recognition as an astonishing feat of creative design. From whatever source materials the physical landscape was derived, naturally they needed to be cartographic rather than textual.

---

[23] We may observe (cf. Weber, loc. cit. in n. 19) that only a slight further increase in length from 855 to 888 cm would bring the map to 30 Roman ft. precisely. There is no knowing what significance, if any, the mapmaker might have attached to the achievement of this round figure. At the least, it is not hard to imagine him welcoming a little extra space at each end, especially to the right, where his design surely incorporated vertical margins (now missing) to complete the frame running along the top and bottom of the map.

[24] In this connection note Salway in Adams and Laurence 2001 (n. 10 above), esp. 54-60.

[25] Note that the only associated feature retained on the London Tube diagram is the R. Thames.

A truly inventive stroke was to reduce bodies of open water to a minimum, retaining enough of them to separate the different land masses from one another, but otherwise freeing up space badly needed for cramming in more land. Even though a distressing amount of the black lettering inscribed over the green water tint has become illegible, it is quite clear that there was a deliberate concern to name bodies of open water, as well as to mark and name many islands, principally within the Mediterranean, although not exclusively. Elsewhere, for example on 10C4, it is striking to see five islands each carefully marked and named within a 'Persian Gulf' to the left of Babylonia (cf. fig. 15). Elevation is not shown with much sophistication. Only the principal mountain ranges and areas of high ground are marked, and even they appear in just a very generalized form. That said, the 'mountain range' symbol does occur very often. Concern to show rivers is more conspicuous, though also uneven across the map. The last type of data to note is cultural, a great variety of names for peoples as well as for regions or provinces. In the case of the latter two especially, widely spaced lettering often requires the eye to follow with care over a considerable distance when identifying a name.[26]

All the physical and cultural data shown, it must be stressed, reflects considered choices on the part of the mapmaker, made in conjunction with the basic design decisions already noted. It surely has to be choice, for instance, that many more peoples are marked to the north and east of the Roman world than to its south in Africa. In any event, the range and quality of source materials at the mapmaker's disposal – wherever he worked – must have been impressive.

Let us turn next to consider (again, briefly) the mapmaker's presentation of data, beginning with the pictorial symbols. The Peutinger map is well known for its attractive range of these, some plainly intended as individual, others more or less standardized. Altogether they mark 557 places or features, not always according to criteria that are self-evident today. The group of baths/spas is readily identifiable,

---

[26] PROVINCIA AFRICA extends furthest, from 2C5 to 6C3. – On my system of references to the Peutinger map see the appendix below.

for example, although questions can be asked about why it was chosen
for inclusion (using such large symbols), as well as how the selection
was made, and from what sources. More generally, it is a puzzle that
certain supposedly insignificant places are given the prominence of a
symbol at all,[27] when some notable cities have none,[28] and others have
a very modest one in relation to their importance.[29]

Rather than pursuing these much-discussed issues here, however, I
turn to a quite different function of the pictorial symbols which seems
to have been overlooked: the role of many (though probably not all) as
'anchors' in establishing the framework for the network of routes (cf.
fig. 16). Consider the likely stages by which a map such as this one is
created.[30] After first settling its intended scope, dimensions and contents, the mapmaker's second step (also large) is surely to lay out the
shorelines and at least the principal rivers and mountain ranges. This
step demands some attention to scale, however variable and imperfect.
The same applies too to the third step, which (I suggest) is to mark in
relation to the physical base those settlements that form the main junctions for the route network that will follow.[31] Also at this third stage, I

[27] For example, Ad Mercurium (3C5), Addianam (8C5).

[28] For example, Casaroduno (1B3), Tergeste (3A5), (H)Aila (8C5, just to the
left of Addianam). In these instances, as in so many others, there is of
course no knowing the degree to which slips or omissions by copyists
have served to transmit the original mapmaker's work inadequately.

[29] For example, Mediolanum (3A2), Chartagine (4C5).

[30] Readers of Weber, *Kommentar* (n. 12 above), 12 – quoted in turn by Brodersen 1995 (n. 9 above), 187 – will realize that my reconstruction here of
the stages by which the map was made is the reverse of theirs, insofar as
they regard the routes as its underpinning and the physical features as, in a
word, 'decoration'. Appropriate demonstration of the falsity of this view
must await the fuller publication I am preparing.

[31] For the most part, a settlement or station where the map user faces a
choice of onward routes is marked by a symbol. That is not necessarily the
case, however, where two routes merely merge (but do not intersect), in
particular when one seems to be only a short link, as between the Sicilibba
and Avitta stretches in 4C4, for example. My formulation 'main junction'
excludes these instances. For an intersection-point not to be marked by a

imagine, the mapmaker may choose to mark with symbols further principal settlements that happen not to be junctions, but are considered of sufficient importance to place in relation to the main junctions.[32]

It is vital to recognize that the only settlements or stations which the mapmaker is prepared to locate specifically are those marked by a symbol (with the name normally written above it, if possible). Otherwise each place just has its name on 'its' stretch of route, followed by the figure which is the distance from there to the next place. Quite deliberately, however, none of these names without a symbol is marked to pinpoint the location of the place. By the same token, the length of the corresponding stretch of route as shown on the map bears no relation to the mileage given for it; the briefest stretch on the map can represent a great distance,[33] a really elongated stretch a very modest one.[34] So, having selected and then marked his 'symbol' settlements (two challenging steps), it only remains for the mapmaker to determine which intermediate places he wants to include, and the distance between each. Scale does not apply, therefore, for everything that lies along the route from one 'symbol' settlement at a main junction to the next. Instead, the length of a stretch is typically determined by nothing more than the combined total of letters in the placename and the distance figure for the stretch.[35]

Finally in this connection we should recognize that it is the mapmaker's aim to write placenames and accompanying distance figures so

symbol is most unusual (but note Dertona in 2B5, for example; in all likelihood Casaroduno in 1B3 was originally marked by a symbol).

[32] Along the upper part of parchment 4 note, for example, Pola, Vindobona (A1), Adprotoriu(m), Sabarie (A2), Brigantio (A3), Aquinco, Sardona (A4), Siscia (A5).

[33] The Chidum (9B1) and Biturs (10B5) stretches, for example.

[34] Several instances in Africa, for example, between 4C2 and 5C5; note also the four miles between Tauruno and Singiduno (5A5-6A1).

[35] Hence on a route where the mapmaker remains determined to mark more intermediate places than his layout can accommodate (rather than selecting only as many as can comfortably fit), an untidy jam results. See, for example, the route between Arelato and Valentia (1B5-2B1).

far as possible in straight horizontal lines, and to draw the corresponding stretches of route likewise. My impression is that in developing the
route network in this way he proceeded – again, so far as possible –
across the map from top to bottom and left to right.[36] Each stretch of
route is defined by a 'chicane' or 'zigzag' at either end,[37] or sometimes
by another route leaving or joining it.[38] Gentle curvature or sloping is
admissible. On occasion, too, routes do proceed at quite a steep
diagonal, but this is normally a last resort, and not to be continued further than necessary. If at all possible, lettering for placenames must
never be placed to overlay road linework, nor must it run into river
courses or open water.

* * * * * * *

The degree of success achieved by this style of presentation is matter for debate. To be sure, if it was the mapmaker's intention to distil
meaningfully into a single, compact map an accumulated mass of purely
written itinerary lists and other such documents – with their inescap-
able overlaps, repetitions, and lack of connections or sense of direction
– then indeed this ambitious goal is achieved, and an entirely new perspective opened up. Even so, the compactness, for all its undoubted
cunning, comes at a price. The placement required for some of the
principal 'symbol' settlements creates a very distorted representation.
Pergamum and Alexandria, for example, lie almost one above the other
on parchment 8 (cf. fig. 17), admittedly with a band of open water in
between; by contrast, Hippo Regius and Carthage lie nearly two parchment-widths apart (3C2-4C5).

---

[36] This is Ptolemy's recommendation, *Geog.* 2.1.5-10 Nobbe = Berggren and
Jones 2000 (n. 16 above), 94-95.

[37] Both terms, as well as the German 'Haken' ('hook') used by Miller, can be
no more than approximations of the mapmaker's practice. My thanks to
Martin Cropp for suggesting 'chicane', a sharp bend designed as a challenge in Formula One motor racing.

[38] See, for example, the Fulgurita (5C5) and Ypepa-Anogome (8B5) stretches.

Even users able to discount such distortions as these could come to regret the additional loss, in effect, of two compass points. Only for general impression is there a north-south dimension to the map. Otherwise the west-east one alone is meaningful, although (again inevitably) what appears to be a west-east route on the map may well not prove to be that on the ground. In North Africa on parchments 1-5, for example, it would be wrong to infer that the five or six routes to be seen forging horizontally in parallel across the map do in fact all proceed thus on the ground; far from it. The same caution applies to the three routes proceeding to the right from Trapezunte (9A2), to cite only one further instance (cf. fig. 18).

So was the Peutinger map intended at all for practical, contemporary use as a route map ? Its presentation definitely gives that impression, and without question there are certain parts which could be used in this way. Even so, altogether it has too many shortcomings to be practical. Travelers who tried to rely on it for making journeys would quickly be liable to encounter puzzles and frustrations.[39] Rather,

---

[39] In our surviving copy at least, there are many instances where no distance figure is attached to a name, as well as many clearly demarcated stretches of route lacking both name and distance figure. It is normally impossible to determine from the map whether such a 'blank' stretch should be ignored as mere embroidery or slip of the pen, or whether travelers would in fact face an indeterminable further distance; for illustration of these dilemmas, see the route Aquileia-Viruno (3A5-4A2). Moreover, in a dismaying number of instances where there is a figure, travelers would hardly feel reassured to read that the distance to the next place is 40, 60, even 100 and more miles – further, in other words, than most travelers would be able to cover in a day or even two. It is true that several of these long intervals occur in remote regions and so may reflect local conditions faithfully enough, but in other instances some shortcoming on the part of the mapmaker could be suspected; note, for example, Casaroduno-Cenabo (1B3-1A3) and Nicopolistro-Marcianopolis (7A2-7A3), each shown as single, unbroken stretches of 51 and 130 respectively. The *Bordeaux Itinerary* is more reassuring by contrast; it seldom advances further than 16 miles or so without recording a road station, often much less, and 24 (once) is its longest interval. In the *Antonine Itinerary* intervals of over 40

I see the users that the mapmaker has in mind as more detached – well-educated aristocrats of the Western empire who, whenever they do travel, leave the practical arrangements to their staff.[40]

The mapmaker's main purpose is to boost such westerners' pride in the range and greatness of Rome's sway historically; hence Milan, Carthage and Alexandria, for example, are all deliberately denied prominence. Only users well grounded in history and geography will properly appreciate the map, whereas others will be confused and misled. At the same time, to a striking degree, its presentation reflects fourth-century intellectual taste in education, art and literature.[41] Higher learning at this period is unashamedly exclusive. Any users of the map who are not already aware that Hippo Regius and Carthage in reality lie closer to one another, and Pergamum and Alexandria much further apart, or that the three routes emerging from Trapezus do not in fact all proceed east, simply reveal their lamentable ignorance. No less pitiful as those who imagine that Herclanium (5B4) and Pompeis (5B5) still exist as marked, or that the Roman road networks shown in Dacia and the Agri Decumates still function.

The better informed, by contrast, may revel in the sheer accumulation of names and details that is so fashionable a feature of fourth-century literature (both prose and poetry), with the added pleasure that many of the names are exotic and 'difficult'. It is a further delight to realize that the placenames and distance figures derive from sources of quite a different type, and are ingeniously re-used here in a fresh, more attractive setting (as was done in 'cento' verse compositions). One can

miles are rare, and most are below 30.

[40] Consider the *nobilitas* of Rome itself, so mercilessly ridiculed by Ammianus Marcellinus not least for their attitude towards travel (28.4.18).

[41] My preliminary treatment of this theme here draws special inspiration from M. Roberts, *The Jeweled Style: Poetry and Poetics in Late Antiquity*, Ithaca and London, 1989. In the same connection, note also R. MacMullen, "Some pictures in Ammianus", chap. 9 in his *Changes in the Roman Empire: Essays in the Ordinary*, Princeton, 1990; and H. Maguire, "The good life", pp. 238-57 in G.W. Bowersock, P. Brown, O. Grabar (eds.), *Late Antiquity: a Guide to the Postclassical World*, Cambridge MA, and London, 1999.

exclaim over the map's format (which is really a text format), so exquisitely compact, with the space so fully used thanks to the deft elimination of most open water and the subtle moulding of landmasses. Certain contrasts seem almost to tease. In some sense there is a discernible north-south dimension, for instance, but altogether it is mostly lacking. Equally, in some respects attention is paid to scale, but in others – as often in works of art – adherence to it is manifestly abandoned. A viewer with the same sense of fun as the writer of the *Historia Augusta* would no doubt be intrigued.

There can be little question that the map in its original form fully reflected the fourth century's love of bright colors.[42] It is tempting to go further and liken its pictorial symbols to the jewels or precious stones (*segmenta*), with which the finest masterpieces of the time were studded for heightened brilliance – most obviously mosaics or monuments, but also (figuratively) poems, and (literally) dress. In this latter regard, the portraits of the two consuls which form part of the Codex-Calendar of 354 are particularly striking (cf. fig. 19). Constantius II alone, as emperor, has jewels on his *toga picta*, but observe the cameo vignettes on that of his colleague Gallus, and the bands or stripes (*clavi*) on both.[43] The Peutinger map in turn can be viewed as a great, long colorful robe or frieze celebrating Rome and Roman power, with the

---

[42] The exceptionally rare occurrence of blue may appear surprising. A blue tint is only to be seen filling the center of some of the large bath/spa symbols (the instances in 6A5 and 9B2 seem clearest, followed perhaps by 6B4). Whether this coloring was original, however, or merely added by a copyist later as an extra flourish, is indeterminable. It could be argued that the mapmaker would hardly have included blue in his palette, only to employ it so little. Alternatively, he may have deliberately kept such flashes of blue to a minimum. Thereby they are rendered all the more conspicuous, and their incorporation into the bath/spa symbols (in turn made large deliberately) would give added pleasure to patrons with a special fondness for such resorts. All water features are otherwise rendered in green.

[43] M.R. Salzman, *On Roman Time: The Codex-Calendar of 354 and the Rhythms of Urban Life in Late Antiquity*, Berkeley, 1990, figs. 13-14.

pictorial symbols as eye-catching *segmenta* and the route linework as *clavi*. Originally, perhaps, the map could just as well have been presented, not on papyrus, but as a wall-painting or tapestry made to resemble a papyrus roll.

Two lesser, related fashions in fourth-century art which it reflects are, first, the fondness for depicting groups of figures who superficially all look alike, but on closer inspection turn out to have different faces or posture or gesture. This superficial sameness that is not necessarily borne out on closer inspection is a feature of the map's pictorial symbols in particular. The second fashion is the predilection for row formation, the organization of groups in ranks, which matches the deliberately 'horizontal' layout of so much of the route network.

More broadly, it is characteristic of a fourth-century work of art (poems, mosaics, buildings both inside and out, etc) to try and make such a dazzling initial impression that readers or viewers actually become disoriented at first. For contemporary taste this is a merit, not a fault. Once recovered, they may turn their attention wherever they wish, and appreciate the work's different elements at their own pace. There ought not to be any dominant element which imposes the adoption of a particular perspective. The Peutinger map fully reflects thinking of this type. It must have been overwhelmingly long, as well as dazzling at first sight. Modern observers have all been conditioned by Miller to focus on the route network as a dominant element, with virtual disregard for everything else. But the fact is that so many more components are present too, both on land and sea. Even the routes themselves are not presented in a prescriptive way. From whatever point on the network users set out, in due course they reach a junction, where typically two or three onward choices are presented. In each such instance users are left completely free to determine their preference. Nothing is done to classify routes by importance, or directness, or any other criterion. Moreover the map offers no figures for the *total* distances between 'symbol' settlements, nor does it mark any boundary-lines (not even between dioceses or empires, let alone provinces). Rather, it consciously appears seamless, uniform, almost unending.

Without question, the Peutinger map will always be extraordinarily important to anyone with an interest in the route network of the

Roman empire and far beyond. But others, too, should take courage to examine it, and to realize how layered a masterpiece it is, capable of being 'read' in a variety of ways and on various levels. As a mirror of its age, it is rewarding not only from a cartographic perspective, but also artistically and intellectually. It deserves to be restored to the cultural mainstream, rather than to remain an isolated curiosity which is typically considered from no more than a single, modern perspective. The 'edition' that I am at present engaged upon is specifically designed to promote greater openness of approach.

The two last words return to the map's cartography, which is so fundamental a component, so woefully neglected to date. First, I now see no means of evading the inference that an ambitious work of such immensity, quality and sophistication could only emerge from an established Roman cartographic tradition; it seems inconceivable for it to have been somehow created almost *ex nihilo*. Of course, at the same time it may be a map that also advances Roman cartography rather than simply demonstrating levels of knowledge and accomplishment already achieved. In any event, the current preference for doubting whether Roman cartography ever attained much development seems overdue for some less skeptical reconsideration. In the same connection, second, students of Roman cartography ought perhaps likewise to be readier to see substance in findings by medievalist colleagues who identify elements in maps of their period as Roman in origin. Such traces of Roman cartography, however imperfectly transmitted, now seem more credible, and they merit systematic search and appraisal.

Appendix: **Reproductions of the map since 1753**

The map's size, color and detail all make it a formidable challenge to reproduce, and study of it has long been impeded as a result. Modern reproductions stem from the full-size engraving published in Vienna by Franz Christoph von Scheyb (1704-77) in 1753. The Bavarian Academy commissioned a reprint made, with some corrections, by Konrad Mannert (1756-1834) in 1824. The map is laid out over 12 doublespreads, a potentially confusing format insofar as a spread is thus slightly less wide than one of the map's 11 parchments.[44]

Ernest Desjardins (1823-86) and Konrad Miller each made the von Scheyb/Mannert engraving the basis of those they were subsequently responsible for, although each also found much fault with it. By the time they inspected the map, it was of course no longer a roll, because (as noted above) the eleven parchment sheets comprising it had been separated in 1863. Desjardins' work was commissioned by the French Ministre de l' Instruction Publique in 1868, although his introductory *Rapport* explains how he had in fact made a first inspection of the map itself the previous year, marking up corrections on a copy of Mannert's engraving.[45] The *Rapport* also includes a careful discussion (p. IV) of how he considered, but ultimately rejected, the idea of commissioning photographs and relying upon them. His work, whose short title is *La Table de Peutinger, d' après l' original conservé à Vienne*, began to appear in 1869 and was eventually planned to comprise 18 livraisons. Only 14

---

[44] Hence the adjective "douze" in the title from the 1960s cited below (n. 65) could mislead the unwary into imagining that a twelfth parchment has come to light!

[45] By this date there was presumably no longer any expectation that Carl Müller (1813-94) would issue the third volume of his *Geographi Graeci Minores*, which had been planned to contain "appendicis loco ... geographi latini, itineraria, tabula Peutingeriana" together with a comprehensive index (*GGM* I [1855], Praefatio, p. V); for Müller's plans, see further the *Introduction générale* to D. Marcotte, *Géographes Grecs* I, Paris, 2000 (Budé series), XIII-XIX.

appeared, however,[46] presumably because the ministry's support came
to be withdrawn.

It was the thorough record of each name and feature, with accompanying commentary, that was cut short. No part of Africa was ever
treated, but otherwise Desjardins did cover everywhere from the
lefthand edge of the map to Sicily inclusive in 254 pages, and had
begun on the names of physical features in *Bassin du Danube et Europe
Orientale* for six pages (255-60), before publication ceased with an
abrupt halt (in mid-word, no less !). Fortunately, however, the entire
map itself had been reproduced by this stage, each parchment appearing full-size as the two halves of a doublespread. The parchments are
numbered from 1 to 11, with three subdivisions marked A, B, C along
the top and bottom, and two marked 1, 2 either side. Desjardins terms
the engraving process a novel one, "chromo-gravure sur pierre", which
was followed by printing in five inks (hence, as he explains, 55 stones
were needed) to create seven colors in all. The result is thus the first
printed representation of the map in color (incorporating even the
original's additional red outline along certain river courses on parchments 1 to 4), and distinctly impressive. In addition, Desjardins offers
three rather elegant maps which trace the Peutinger map's routes on
standard modern outlines of northern Italy (to Rome),[47] southern Italy
and Sicily,[48] and Gaul.[49]

Even so, the expense and incompleteness of Desjardins' full work
were two obvious obstacles to his representation ever gaining the

[46] 7 livraisons in 1869, 2 in 1870, 2 in 1872 after publication had been
"interrompue par les événements", 1 in 1873, 2 in 1874.

[47] Doublespread at 1:1,923,000, with inset *Submoenium Urbis* at 1:580,000
(figures in this note and the two following are rounded approximations
calculated from the scalebar on each map; the maps themselves offer no
figures).

[48] Doublespread at 1:1,923,000, with inset *Campaniae Pars Media* at 1:455,000.

[49] Single turn-page at 1:4,545,500; this map is reprinted in Desjardins'
Géographie historique et administrative de la Gaule romaine IV, 1893, facing p.
76, on which see further below.

prominence it deserved.[50] Instead, the engraving *Die Peutingersche Tafel* published by Miller eclipsed it, and still remains in use today. As a teacher devoted to making the map widely accessible at an affordable price, Miller would no doubt have been very satisfied by this outcome. His VIII 5 to XII 5 (identical copies of the 1962 edition, on which see further below) form the principal feature of *TAVO* B S 1 *Weltkarten der Antike/Ancient Maps of the World*, 1.2 *Tabula Peutingeriana*, with accompanying text by J. Wagner (1984). His engraving is recommended by Salway in Adams and Laurence 2001,[51] and featured throughout that book. It was also the choice for display in the major exhibit *Segni e Sogni della Terra* (Milan, 2001).[52]

Its first appearance was in 1888, in conjunction with a book ("Einleitender Text," 128 pp.), *Die Weltkarte des Castorius*, dated the previous year. Miller promotes it as a substantial revision of von Scheyb's work. The representation is a single piece in color, with a format approximately two-thirds of the original map's size. The points where each of the parchments join are indicated, with the latter numbered II to XII (reflecting the assumption that one more beyond the lefthand edge is missing), and each subdivided 1, 2, 3, 4, 5 along the top, but without any corresponding subdivision either side. Along the bottom, at the appropriate spots below selected ancient names marked on the map, is added in italic the modern equivalent name for each. Here, too, in standard type, is added the ancient name (as inferred by Miller) for many of the unnamed symbols on the map.

The same single-piece representation *Die Peutingersche Tafel* was reissued in the year (1916) that Miller's *Itineraria Romana* appeared. I believe it is correct to claim that any purchaser of the latter would only want the *Tafel* too for the impact that a single piece creates, because otherwise the materials in it and the volume effectively match. By comparison with the 1888 version, however, there is the double dis-

---

[50] Miller (*Die Weltkarte des Castorius*, 3) quotes a price of 140 francs for the map facsimile in 1887.

[51] Adams and Laurence 2001 (n. 10 above), 60 n. 2.

[52] But not for the catalog, on which see further below.

appointment that in both 1916 publications the representation is further reduced to approximately half the original map's size, and it also lacks color. At least the two types of name added along the bottom not only reappear in *Die Peutingersche Tafel*, but are also revised for it. In addition, its purchaser now gains a substantial introductory text (16 pp.), followed by 12 pages of route sketch maps either reproduced from, or derived from, *Itineraria Romana*.[53] A further 'bonus' in both publications is the inclusion of Miller's imaginative reconstruction of the single parchment that in his view served to complete the lefthand side of the map. When originally issued in 1898, this measured 40 x 22 cm, and appeared in blue, light-brown and black.[54] Reduced in size and lacking color, it is now integrated into the single-piece representation for *Die Peutingersche Tafel* with modern equivalent names added along the bottom, while segments of most of it (but not the far left) appear in *Itineraria Romana*.[55]

The 1916 version of *Die Peutingersche Tafel* was reprinted without alteration in 1929,[56] and again in 1962.[57] In the latter instance, however, color was returned to most of the map, reproducing the palette used in 1888; only the reconstructed lefthand parchment remains black and white. Outdated though many of the modern toponyms along the bottom might seem by 1962 in particular, they were not revised (a task

---

[53] I = *ItRom* 5-6, 947-48; II = 33-34; III = 147-48; IV = 195-96; V = 197-98; VI = 413-14; VII = 497-98; VIII = 566, 542; IX = 629-30, plus *Libyen und Tripolis* derived from *ItRom* chaps. XI and XII; X = 751-52; XI = 753-54, 789, plus *Agypten* derived from 859-66; XII = 885-86, plus *Algier und Oran* derived from 913-14.

[54] See n. 18 above.

[55] 3-4, 27, 147-49, 887-88, 946.

[56] On the front cover: "2. unveränderte Auflage." In X 5 of the 1916 version, the spelling DIVALIMUEETICE seems a curiosity. In all other versions both earlier and later, and in *ItRom* 635-36, it is DIVALIMUSETICE.

[57] Note that the sheets gummed together to form the single-piece map are a longer size in 1962.

that would have brought with it the additional complication of altering the text too, wherever these names are mentioned).[58]

Despite its continuing availability and undoubted improvement on von Scheyb's work, Miller's *Die Peutingersche Tafel* should not be regarded as an infallibly reliable reproduction of the map. Glaring errors or omissions seem rare, to be sure; omission of the route connecting Augusta Taurinor(um) and the Eporedia stretch (III 5) is an exceptional oversight, therefore. There are several smaller discrepancies, however. In at least two instances, Miller's engraver – working from von Scheyb's reproduction but creating plates of different length – evidently failed to achieve a smooth continuation between a pair of his predecessor's adjoining plates. In consequence, at Miller's V 4 the lettering for THURRIS becomes jumbled; the Risca stretch has an extra chicane added to it; the 'S' and 'eggo' of Seggo are separated; 'Mil(ia) XVIIII' is placed too far left, and an extra chicane is introduced after it; likewise the Speculum stretch acquires an extra chicane. Similar errors are introduced into Miller's XI 2 for the same reason. The righthand parts of all three 'special notices' stand lower than they should, and 'inopiam' has even acquired an additional (redundant) 'i'; the name Metita is spread over two road stretches, when there should only be one.[59]

Color is an integral part of the map's presentation, and any user of the 1916 or 1929 reproductions (including *ItRom*) is deprived of that vital aspect.[60] Moreover the deprivation extends beyond the obvious. For example, the lack of color renders it impossible to distinguish confidently between islands drawn on the map and holes in the parchment. It is true that Miller may confirm an unnamed island to be such

---

[58] *TAVO* B S 1.1.2 chooses not to reproduce Miller's names along the bottom. Instead, certain ancient names on the map that may give the reader difficulty are spelled out here (in capital and lower case lettering), while ancient names (in all capitals) are supplied for certain unnamed symbols.

[59] At both joins cited, Desjardins' engraver made smoother continuations, except that he, too, spreads the name Metita over two road stretches.

[60] Like Desjardins, Miller (1888) even marks the additional red outline along certain river courses.

by adding 'Ins.' next to it (as in his IX 5), but not invariably. Thus users might assume there to be a sequence of three holes in his IX 2-3; in fact only the furthest right of the three is a hole, and the other two are islands. By contrast, above Pyreo in his VIII 1 are simply to be seen one small and one large hole; neither is an island.

It was perhaps inevitable that Miller's engraving should present much lettering with a greater degree of confidence than a cautious reader of the map itself might share. In fact it became possible to make extensive comparison without the need to visit Vienna from 1888, when a set of eleven full-size monochrome photographs by the respected Viennese firm of Angerer and Göschl was published. Each photograph is mounted on a loose card, and numbered Segmentum I-XI. A title card (*Peutingeriana Tabula Itineraria in Bibliotheca Palatina Vindobonensi asservata nunc primum arte photographica expressa*), and a folder-case of heavy board with the first three words of the title stamped in gold on the front, are the sole accompanying components. The remarkable quality of the photographer's work in fact makes this set quite indispensable for reading any lettering marked on land, although my impression is that the photographs have never been accorded the attention they merit.

Two main reasons are readily identified. First, Miller preferred to place reliance upon the engraving that he had been responsible for himself; this was ill-advised perhaps, but understandable. My impression, at least, is that in *ItRom* his discussion of problems seldom refers explicitly to the 1888 photographs.[61] He believed that in any case it was more important to take note of what the map's earliest engravers had recorded – lettering or other data that was reckoned to have since faded from view.[62] Second, the set of photographs seems to have been extraordinarily expensive. In 1916, in *ItRom* (XXVI), Miller quotes its price as 165 Marks, at the same time as *ItRom* is offered in two differ-

[61] For an instance, note the entry for Gerainas, 136 and n. 1.
[62] *ItRom* XXVI; Weber, *Kommentar* 7, is of course only right to repeat Kubitschek's warning that such 'faded' material may more often have been imagined than seen.

ent bindings for 32 or 36 Marks. Few libraries acquired the set, therefore; and of those that did, even fewer have been willing to lend such
an item.

One or more photographs presumably from this set have appeared
in later publications, with (as it happens) steadily decreasing reduction
in size. Segmentum I at full size forms the foldout plate IX (facing p.
72) in the fourth and last volume of Desjardins' *Géographie historique et
administrative de la Gaule romaine*, published posthumously in 1893. The
full set of eleven, each reduced to approximately three-quarters full-
size, is reproduced first in Youssouf Kamal's *Monumenta Cartographica
Africae et Aegypti* tome 2 fasc. 2 (Cairo, 1932), 234-37;[63] but this
incomparably large, lavish and rare publication hardly increased aware-
ness of the photographs. The full set is appended next to A. and M.
Levi, *Itineraria Picta* (Rome, 1967) as eleven pull-out plates; the reduction in size is considerable, however (40 x 22 cm), and the quality of
the images disappointing. The full set is appended last to L. Bosio, *La
Tabula Peutingeriana* (Rimini, 1983), with a better quality of image, but
each parchment shrunk to no more than approximately 26 x 14 cm so
as to fit the book's page-size.[64]

Amazingly, after the 1880s it was to be almost another century
before new reproductions of the map appeared.[65] Then, ironically, two

[63] Note that there then follow reproductions of the first complete publication
of the map by M. Welser (1598), and of Miller's reconstruction of the
missing lefthand parchment; the latter, lacking color, is in fact slightly
larger than in its original publication.

[64] The fifty or so color reproductions from the map interspersed through the
main body of this book (of all shapes and sizes, both reduced and
enlarged) are far more successful and useful, although a checklist is lacking.

[65] Although my efforts to trace it have so far failed, I can hardly think that
the work mentioned by R. Chevallier, *Roman Roads* (California, 1976), 231
was new: "A popular edition, *Les Douze Segments de la Table de Peutinger*, has
been issued by the Société Gaule, 10, Paris (based on von Scheyb)." I take
this to be the 1965 work reported by A. and M. Levi (who likewise had
not seen it), *Itineraria Picta*, 18.

sets of color photographs were published in quick succession and (it seems) quite independently of one another. The earlier set, issued from Graz with a *Kommentar* book by E. Weber in 1976,[66] is of better quality. There is a full-size photograph for each parchment, and the eleven are bound as a book which opens upwards. Above each of these color photographs (and thus on the reverse of the preceding page) there appears a duplicate image, but monochrome, and with approximately 2 to 7 cm of the preceding and following parchments placed immediately adjacent on either side (marked off by white dividing lines). The lines for Miller's five sub-divisions of each parchment are also drawn on these monochrome photographs; in addition, the (up-to-date) modern equivalent name of each place marked by a symbol is given, printed in white over the symbol or close by. Weber likewise suggests a reading for those ancient names marked on open water which give special difficulty; for the most part he adopts Miller's reading.[67] Unfortunately in some instances the overprinting of these suggestions hinders users who want to make their own reading of a poorly preserved name by examining the relevant black-and-white photograph as well as the color one.

The special merit of the second set of color photographs – one for each parchment in fact, full-size, published by A. and M. Levi in 1978 (Edizioni Edison, Bologna) – is that they are gummed together to present the map in its original, single-piece format. A wooden roller is attached at each end to form a scroll. The result is predictably memorable. At the same time, however, there are disappointments. The photographs lack the sharpness of Weber's, and (since they are to be rolled up) the paper on which they are printed is less sturdy. Moreover the lavishness of the production – the scroll lies in a casket with an accompanying book *La "Tabula Peutingeriana"* – seems to have deterred

[66] Note also the undated re-issue by Edizioni U.C.T. Trento, accompanied only by a single-sided information-sheet (in Italian) in place of the *Kommentar*. Prof. Weber kindly informs me that he currently has a new edition of his entire work (both maps and commentary) in preparation.

[67] Not invariably, however; the conjecture 'Ins. Ṭạl[artica?],' for example, exceeds even *ItRom* 851 for boldness.

most libraries from acquiring this set of photographs in addition to Weber's.

At some date since these published sets of color photographs were taken during the 1970s, two developments have occurred which notably affect the reproduction of the maps. First, varying degrees of darkening have been applied to most (though not quite all) holes or gashes in the parchments. Previously, since the backing to which the parchments are attached is white, it was easy to distinguish holes or gashes. Now, in more recent photographs, it can be awkward. The slightly reduced image of part of parchment 9 which forms p. 38 in the exhibit catalog *Segni e Sogni della Terra* (Milan, 2001) illustrates the difficulty: compare the area of open water below Insula Cypros with its appearance in the 1888 photograph or those of Weber.[68]

Second, each parchment has been placed in a plastic case from which it cannot be removed, and through which all photographs must therefore now be taken. Unfortunately for this purpose, there are air-holes in the clear plastic top of the case, placed every 8 cm horizontally and every 7 cm vertically. At times, inevitably, the placement of an air-hole hinders close examination of a detail, while the shadow it may cast can also prove a distraction.[69] The air-holes show up throughout the set of eleven scanned images (one for each parchment) which the National Library, Vienna, has recently consented to make available under certain conditions.[70]

Miller has remained alone in his numbering of the parchments as 2-12 rather than 1-11. On the other hand, his vertical subdivision of each

---

[68] The point also applies left and right of Insula Rhodos on the same parchment, although this p. 38 does not extend so far. In addition, p. 37 offers miniature, but clear, color images of parchments 1-8 (with 6 and 1 needing to be transposed).

[69] See in general *Segni e Sogni della Terra*, 38, where the air-holes and (along the bottom in particular) their shadows are clearly visible.

[70] Hence, on this scan, the red Q of QUADI in 3A5 gives the impression of over-writing a black letter, which turns out to be merely the shadow cast by an air-hole. Similarly, in 10B5, the hope that a distance figure may in fact follow the name Sapham is false for the same reason.

one into five has become standard. Weber (*Kommentar* 43), who returned to numbering the parchments as I-XI, recognized the need for horizontal subdivisions too. He uses three – 'o(ben), m(itte), u(nten)' – in his Register, although he never incorporates the corresponding demarcation lines in any of his photographs. My own practice is to number the parchments 1-11, to retain Miller's vertical subdivisions (referred to by number, 1-5), and to demarcate three horizontal ones referred to by letter, A, B, C. Unlike Miller, I follow the map number with the letter for the horizontal subdivision, and then the number for the vertical one. Thus, for example, Perintus (which is in VIII 5 in Miller and VII 5 m in Weber) is in 7B5 by my system.

In recent decades the National Library, Vienna, has understandably been concerned at the risk of further deterioration to the map's condition. As a result, it has not been publicly displayed, and even scholars' access to it has been very much restricted.[71] Just when the map was withdrawn from public view, I have yet to determine, however. Later than October 21, 1924, it would seem, to judge by the report of an unnamed 'special correspondent' who wrote an article for the *Christian Science Monitor* (Boston) that day, preserved by the New York Public Library Map Division. It explains the attraction of the map and concludes: "To the student of the Roman period, this 'Peutinger Table' would be of particular interest; and, even for the ordinary traveler to Vienna, it is well worth the climb up three winding flights of stone stairs to see."[72]

---

[71] Note the experience of A. and M. Levi, *La "Tabula Peutingeriana"* 9.

[72] Except for the 1888 photographs, the New York Public Library happens to hold all the items cited in this Appendix; my thanks to Alice C. Hudson (Chief, Map Division) for assistance there. The Ancient World Mapping Center, UNC, Chapel Hill (www.unc.edu/awmc), holds scanned images of the 1888 photographs, on which our figs. 13-19 are based.

Figures

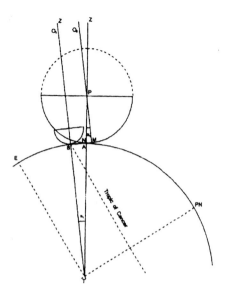

fig. 1 Eratosthenes' method of determining the circumference of the earth.

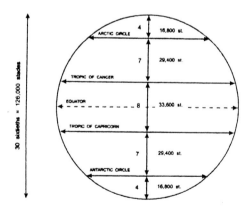

fig. 2 An attempt at reconstructing Eratosthenes' model of the earth.

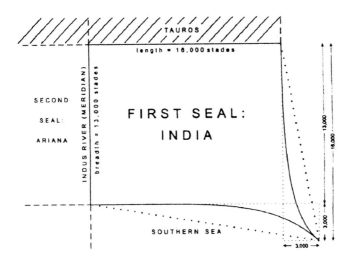

fig. 3 An attempt at reconstructing Eratosthenes' "first seal".

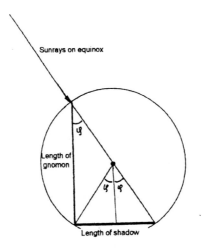

fig. 4 Use of a table of chords for the calculation of latitude φ with a gnomon (a horizontal sundial). The length of the shadow equals a chord of 2φ, the height of the gnomon a chord of $180° - 2φ$.

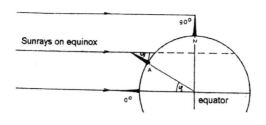

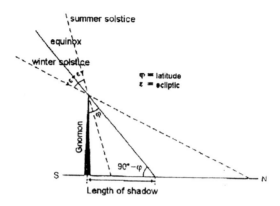

fig. 5 Measuring the latitude φ with the gnomon: at noon of the equinox the relation of the length of the shadow to the height of the gnomon is tan φ .

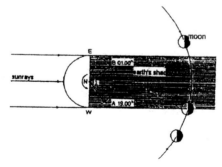

fig. 6 Observation of a lunar eclipse to calculate longitude according to Ptol. geogr. 1, 4, 2. For example, if in A the shadow of the earth hits the moon at 19.00 local time, in B at 01.00 local time, the difference of 6 hours allows to conclude a difference in longitude of 90° .

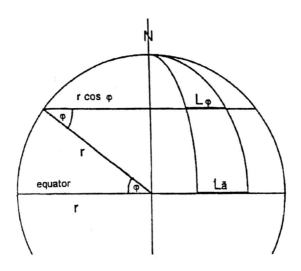

fig. 7 The 'shortening' of longitudinal degrees in relation to degrees of latitude: longitudinal degree φ = equatorial degree x cos φ .

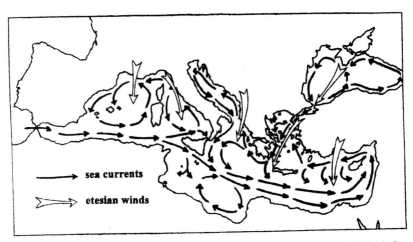

fig. 8 Surface currents and etesian winds in the Mediterranean and Black Sea during the sailing season.

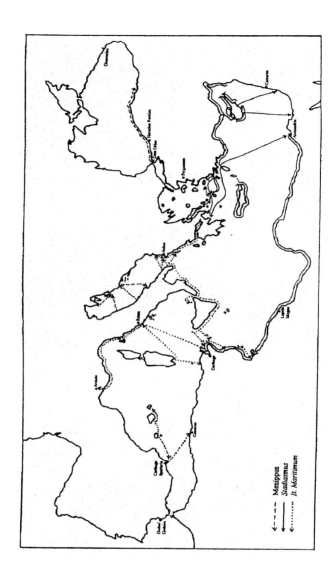

fig. 9 Coverage of the Mediterranean and Black Sea by the extant portions of Menippus' *Periplus* and the *Stadiasmus maris magni* and of the *Itinerarium Maritimum (Itinerarium Antonini).*

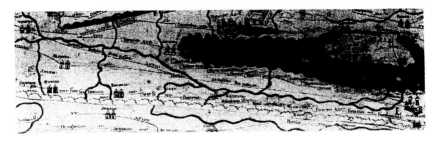

fig. 10 *Tabula Peutingeriana* III 5 m / 3B5: the stretch Hostilia – Ravenna *per padum*.

fig. 11 *Tabula Peutingeriana* IX 1-2 m / 9B1-2: the stretch Miletus – Patara.

fig. 12 The Dura Parchment.

fig. 13 Representative segment of the *Tabula Peutingeriana* (righthand end of parchment 2, showing margins top and bottom).

fig. 14 Lefthand end of the *Tabula Peutingeriana* as it survives (parchment 1).

fig. 15 The 'Persian Gulf' and its five islands on the *Tabula Peutingeriana* (parchment 10).

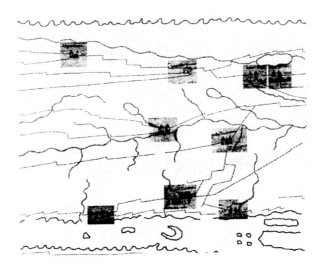

fig. 16 Shoreline, rivers, route linework and pictorial symbols on a segment of the *Tabula Peutingeriana* (parchment 2) corresponding to fig. 13.

fig. 17 Segment of the *Tabula Peutingeriana* (parchment 8) showing the relationship of Pergamum and Alexandria (unnamed symbol at the lefthand end of the Nile delta).

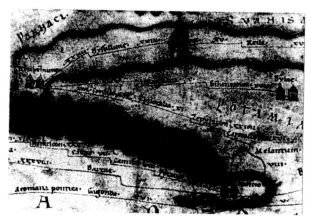

fig. 18 The three routes from Trapezunte on the *Tabula Peutingeriana* (parchment 9).

fig. 19 Constantius II and Gallus as consuls in the *Calendar of 354*.

Wissenschaftliche Paperbacks

Geschichtswissenschaft

Michael Richter

Irland im Mittelalter

Kultur und Geschichte

Im Mittelalter erlebte Irland eine frühe kulturelle Blüte, von der heute noch prachtvolle Handschriften wie das „Book of Kelts" oder die vielen Klosterruinen auf der „Grünen Insel" Zeugnis ablegen. Der Konstanzer Historiker Michael Richter hat eine kurze Geschichte dieser ereignisreichen Jahrhunderte geschrieben, die dem am Mittelalter interessierten Leser ebenso nachdrücklich empfohlen werden kann wie dem Irlandliebhaber.

Bd. 16, 2003, 216 S., 18,80 €, br., ISBN 3-8258-6437-5

Geschichte: Forschung und Wissenschaft

Kersten Krüger; Gyula Pápay; Stefan Kroll (Hg.)

Stadtgeschicht und Historische Informationssysteme

Der Ostseeraum im 17. und 18. Jahrhundert. Beiträge des wissenschaftlichen Kolloquiums in Rostock vom 21. und 22. März 2002

Die modernen multimedialen Technologien eröffnen auch der Geschichtswissenschaft zunehmend neue Forschungsperspektiven. Dies verdeutlicht der vorliegende Sammelband am Beispiel der Stadtgeschichte des Ostseeraums im 17. und 18. Jahrhundert. Die mit zahlreichen Abbildungen versehenen Beiträge von 14 Autoren aus sechs Ländern leisten eine Verbindung zwischen methodischer Innovation und empirischer Forschung. Dem Band beigefügt ist eine CD-ROM, die das multimediale Historische Informationssystem „Wohnen und Wirtschaften in Stralsund um 1700" (u. a. mit 66 sozialtopographischen Karten) enthält.

Bd. 1, 2003, 328 S., 24,90 €, br., ISBN 3-8258-7103-7

Ivo Asmus; Heiko Droste; Jens E. Olesen (Hg.)

Gemeinsame Bekannte

Schweden und Deutschland in der Frühen Neuzeit

Die schwedisch-deutsche Geschichte der Frühen Neuzeit hat viele Facetten. Der militärischen Eroberung Pommerns, Bremen-Verdens und Wismars folgte ein reger Austausch von Beamten, Kaufleuten, Künstlern und Militärs. Diese Gemeinsamen Bekannten stehen im Mittelpunkt des vorliegenden Bandes, der die positiven wie negativen Aspekte der deutsch-schwedischen Geschichte untersucht. Die Autoren sind ausgewiesene Kenner der schwedisch-deutschen Geschichte, die in ihren Aufsätzen quellennahe und aktuelle Forschungsergebnisse aus schwedischer, dänischer und deutscher Perspektive bieten.

Bd. 2, 2003, 448 S., 34,90 €, br., ISBN 3-8258-7150-9

Antike Kultur und Geschichte

herausgegeben von Prof. Dr. Kai Brodersen
(Universität Mannheim)

Kai Brodersen (Hg.)

Gebet und Fluch, Zeichen und Traum

Aspekte religiöser Kommunikation in der Antike

Die Lebenswelten der Antike sind in vielfältiger Weise von religiöser Kommunikation geprägt. In Untersuchungen von Kai Brodersen (Mannheim/Newcastle), Veit Rosenberger (Augsburg/Atlanta), Jörg Rüpke (Erfurt), Tanja S. Scheer (München) und Gregor Weber (Eichstätt/Erfurt) zu Gebet und Fluch, Zeichen und Traum will der Band Aspekte religiöser Kommunikation in antiken Staatswesen erhellen und anhand eines systematisch wenig beachteten Bereichs antiker Mentalitäten zu Erkenntnissen über die historische Anthropologie antiker Gesellschaften und der in ihnen gegebenen Handlungsräume beitragen.

Bd. 1, 2001, 120 S., 17,90 €, br., ISBN 3-8258-5352-7

Kai Brodersen (Hg.)

Prognosis

Studien zur Funktion von Zukunftsvorhersagen in Literatur und Geschichte seit der Antike

Prognosis – das Bemühen um "Vorwissen" durch Zukunftsvorhersagen begegnet uns seit dem Beginn der schriftlichen Überlieferung. Julia Kindt (Cambridge), Sjoerd Levelt (Amsterdam), Michael Maaß (Karlsruhe), Daniel Ogden (Swansea), Karen Piepenbrink (Mannheim), Veit Rosenberger (Atlanta) und Tanja S. Scheer (München)

LIT Verlag Münster – Hamburg – Berlin – Wien – London
Grevener Str./Fresnostr. 2 48159 Münster
Tel.: 0251 – 23 50 91 – Fax: 0251 – 23 19 72
e-Mail: vertrieb@lit-verlag.de – http://www.lit-verlag.de

untersuchen in ihren Beiträgen die Funktion von Zukunftsvorhersagen in Literatur und Geschichte seit der Antike. Der Bogen der Studien reicht dabei von der Pythia von Delphi über die griechischen Totenorakel bis zu Merlin und von Homer und Herodot über die christliche Spätantike bis in die mittelalterliche Geschichtsschreibung und zur neugriechischen Dichtung.
Bd. 2, 2001, 144 S., 20,90 €, br., ISBN 3-8258-5341-1

J. Manuel Schulte
Speculum Regis
Studien zur Fürstenspiegel-Literatur in der griechisch-römischen Antike
Fürstenspiegel bringt man meist mit dem Mittelalter und der Neuzeit in Verbindung, doch beschreibt der Begriff ein bereits im Altertum bekanntes Phänomen: Wo nämlich Macht ausgeübt wird, gab es immer ein Bedürfnis, Machthabern Maßstäbe, Spielregeln und Grundtugenden ihrer Position zu erklären. Die vorliegende Arbeit hat es sich zur Aufgabe gemacht, die Fürstenspiegel-Literatur der griechisch-römischen Antike zu untersuchen. Sie beginnt dabei mit den homerischen Epen und endet mit Mark Aurels Selbstbetrachtungen. Aus einer Quellenschau heraus will die Arbeit die Art, Ausprägung und Entwicklung der antiken Fürstenspiegel-Literatur darlegen und erläutern.
Bd. 3, 2001, 296 S., 25,90 €, br., ISBN 3-8258-5249-0

Kai Brodersen (Hg.)
Die Antike außerhalb des Hörsaals
„Die Antike außerhalb der Hörsaals"? Begegnet uns die Welt des Altertums denn nicht nur im Studium? Ja! An einem ganzen Strauß von Beispielen zeigen die in diesem Band gesammelten Beiträge, wie präsent die Antike auch und gerade außerhalb des Hörsaals ist: auf der Bühne und im Nationaldenkmal, in der Kinder- und Jugendliteratur, in Kino und Krimi – aber auch im Flugblatt der *Weißen Rose*.
Der Band enthält Beiträge von Kai Brodersen, Stefanie Eichler, Nadia Endl, Daniela Evers, Rosmarie Günther, Niklas Holzberg, Stefan Kipf, Ralf Krebs und Susanna Phillippo.
Bd. 4, 2003, 176 S., 19,90 €, br., ISBN 3-8258-6852-4

Schriften zur Geschichte des Altertums

Wolfram Letzner
Lucius Cornelius Sulla
Versuch einer Biographie
Das vorliegende Buch stellt den Versuch dar, L. Cornelius Sulla, eine der herausragendsten Persönlichkeiten der späten römischen Republik, in seinem historischen Umfeld vorzustellen. Die Beurteilung Sullas in der Vergangenheit schwankt zwischen Bewunderung und harscher Kritik, die dieser Persönlichkeit weder in der einen noch der anderen Richtung gerecht werden. Hier wird ein Gratwanderung unternommen, die zu einem neutraleren Bild führen soll.
Bd. 1, 2000, 368 S., 61,90 €, gb., ISBN 3-8258-5041-2

Vita regularis
Ordnungen und Deutungen religiosen Lebens im Mittelalter
herausgegeben von Prof. Dr. Gert Melville
(Technische Universität Dresden)

Gert Melville (Hg.)
De ordine vitae
Zu Normvorstellungen, Organisationsformen und Schriftgebrauch im mittelalterlichen Ordenswesen
Bd. 1, 1996, 400 S., 35,90 €, br., ISBN 3-8258-2586-8

Jörg Oberste
Visitation und Ordensorganisation
Formen sozialer Normierung, Kontrolle und Kommunikation bei Cisterziensern, Prämonstratensern und Cluniazensern (12. – frühes 14. Jahrhundert)
Bd. 2, 1996, 472 S., 35,90 €, br., ISBN 3-8258-2587-6

Godula Süßmann
Konflikt und Konsens
Zu den Auseinandersetzungen zwischen cluniazensischen Klöstern und ihren rechtsabhängigen burgenses im Frankreich des 12. und 13. Jahrhunderts
Bd. 3, 1997, 400 S., 24,90 €, br., ISBN 3-8258-2588-4

LIT Verlag Münster – Hamburg – Berlin – Wien – London
Grevener Str./Fresnostr. 2 48159 Münster
Tel.: 0251 – 23 50 91 – Fax: 0251 – 23 19 72
e-Mail: vertrieb@lit-verlag.de – http://www.lit-verlag.de

Kay Peter Jankrift
Leprose als Streiter Gottes
Institutionalisierung und Organisation des
Ordens vom heiligen Lazarus zu Jerusalem
von seinen Anfängen bis zum Jahre 1350
Im Mittelpunkt der Studie steht die organisa-
torische und institutionelle Entwicklung einer
Leprosenbruderschaft außerhalb der Mauern
Jerusalems zum Orden des Heiligen Lazarus.
Vor dem Hintergrund einer Zeit, die als einzi-
ge Antwort auf die Schrecken der unheilbaren
Lepra den mit Entrechtung und Stigmatisierung
einhergehenden Ausschluß des Erkrankten aus
der Welt der Gesunden kannte, entwirft sie das
Porträt einer außergewöhnlichen, von der historischen Forschung bislang weitgehend unbeachteten
Gemeinschaft. Beschränkten sich die Lazariter
anfangs auf die materielle und spirituelle Ver-
sorgung ihrer kranken Brüder, so ließen sie sie
schon bald aktiv teilhaben an der bedeutendsten
Mission der mittelalterlichen Christenheit: dem
Kampf um das Heilige Land. Neben der Entfal-
tung des Ordens in den Kreuzfahrerstaaten gilt
die Untersuchung jedoch auch dem Schicksal
der europäischen Lazariterhäuser. Die Ausbil-
dung seiner hierarchischen Strukturen wird dabei
ebenso analysiert wie seine normativen Texte, die
mit denen anderer Ritterorden und den Statuten
europäischer Leprosorien verglichen werden.
Schließlich wendet sich die Studie unter Berücksichtigung der ökonomischen Ressourcen der
Lazariter und der allgemeinen leprosenrechtlichen
Entwicklung der Frage nach der militärischen und
hospitalischen Bedeutung des Ordens zu.
Bd. 4, 1997, 272 S., 30,90 €, br., ISBN 3-8258-2589-2

Clemens M. Kasper; Klaus Schreiner (Hrsg.)
Viva vox und ratio scripta
Mündliche und schriftliche
Kommunikationsformen im Mönchtum des
Mittelalters
Mit Beiträgen von Arnold Angenendt, Karl Suso
Frank, Clemens Kasper, Franz Neiske, Klaus
Schreiner u. a.
Bd. 5, 1997, 320 S., 35,90 €, br., ISBN 3-8258-2950-2

Burkhardt Tutsch
**Studien zur Rezeptionsgeschichte der
Consuetudines Ulrichs von Cluny**
Zum Ende des 11. Jahrhunderts hin hielt der
cluniacensische Mönch Ulrich den normativen
Anspruch vorbildlichen klösterlichen Lebens in
Cluny in einer umfangreichen Sammlung von
Consuetudines fest. Diese verschriftlichten Le-
bensgewohnheiten wurden von Konventen in
ganz Europa als Orientierung für das eigene
monastische Leben erbeten. Der vorliegende Band
untersucht ausgehend von den erhaltenen Hand-
schriften der Consuetudines an Beispielen aus
Frankreich, Italien und Deutschland, wie die am
Lebensideal Clunys interessierten Konvente mit
dem ihnen gelieferten Text tatsächlich umgingen
und welche Konsequenzen der Rezeptionsprozeß
für die Ausformung ihres eigenen klösterlichen
Lebens hatte.
Bd. 6, 1998, 440 S., 40,90 €, br., ISBN 3-8258-3200-7

Giles Constable; Gert Melville;
Jörg Oberste (Hrsg.)
**Die Cluniazenser in ihrem politisch-
sozialen Umfeld**
Die Mönche von Cluny suchten, dem benedikti-
nischen Ideal folgend, ihren Weg zu Gott hinter
Klostermauern und veränderten dabei die Welt
jenseits dieser Mauern. Mit der Frage der Einbet-
tung der cluniazensischen Konvente und Klöster
in die politischen und sozialen Strukturen ihrer
Umgebung befassen sich in dem vorliegenden
Band 19 Cluny-Forscher aus 5 Ländern. Sie
bieten die zu diesem Thema bislang einzige Zu-
sammenschau systematischer, geographischer und
diachroner Aspekte: angefangen bei Problemen
der Gründung, über die wirtschaftlichen, sozialen,
politischen und kulturellen Beziehungen zu den
Mächten des regionalen Umfelds, bis hin zu der
Integration in das Corpus der Universalkirche und
der Ausbreitung Clunys im christlichen Europa.
Dort, wo Antagonismen und Konflikte vorherr-
schen, scheint die Opposition Kloster-Welt am
lebendigsten; in anderen Fällen dringen die säku-
laren Bedürfnisse tief bis in das klaustrale Leben
ein. Gleichwohl lösen die hier versammelten
Beiträge eine solche Opposition gerade dort auf,
wo man auf das unverwechselbar Monastische zu
stoßen scheint: Das klösterliche Totengedenken
etwa, höchster Ausdruck der cluniazensischen
Spiritualität, war zugleich der wohl wichtigste
Berührungspunkt mit den religiösen und sozialen
Bedürfnissen des adlig-laikalen Umfelds.
Bd. 7, 1998, 596 S., 40,90 €, br., ISBN 3-8258-3441-7

LIT Verlag Münster – Hamburg – Berlin – Wien – London
Grevener Str./Fresnostr. 2 48159 Münster
Tel.: 0251 – 23 50 91 – Fax: 0251 – 23 19 72
e-Mail: vertrieb@lit-verlag.de – http://www.lit-verlag.de

Anette Kehnel
Clonmacnois – the Church and Lands of St. Ciarán
Change and Continuity in an Irish Monastic Foundation (6th to 16th Century)
Clonmacnois was one of the main ecclesiastical centres in early Christian Ireland. Yet no comprehensive work has hitherto been published which examines its history as an institution of religious, social and economic life. This book undertakes a detailed analysis of Clonmacnois before and during the age of reform and assesses possible reasons for its subsequent decline as an ecclesiastical centre. It traces the history of the former lay-ecclesiastical aristocracy down to the later Middle Ages, and, using previously neglected evidence surviving in seventeenth-century transcripts, sets out to reconstruct the extent of the former monastic lands.
Bd. 8, 1998, 368 S., 30,90 €, br., ISBN 3-8258-3442-5

Thomas Füser
Mönche im Konflikt
Zum Spannungsfeld von Norm, Devianz und Sanktionen bei den Cisterziensern und Cluniazensern (12. bis frühes 14. Jahrhundert)
Das Spannungsfeld von Norm und Devianz ist nicht nur ein Kernproblem sozialer Ordnungen überhaupt, sondern tangiert darüber hinaus wesentliche Kategorien religioser Lebensformen. Die mittelalterlichen Orden gaben dem Wechselspiel von Norm, Devianz und Sanktion einen neuen, festen institutionellen Rahmen. Statutenwerke, Generalkapitelbeschlüsse und Visitationsprotokolle ermöglichen eine eingehende Analyse. Gerade die elementaren monastischen Verhaltensforderungen können zugleich als zentrale Problemfelder individueller klösterlicher Lebensführung beschrieben werden: Verstöße gegen *pax* und *oboedientia*, Abweichungen im Zusammenhang mit dem Keuschheitsgelübde, Diebstahl und Eigenbesitz und schließlich Formen der Flucht aus dem Kloster. Die Darstellung verfolgt jeweils das Ziel, einen engen Konnex herzustellen zwischen den positivrechtlichen Normierungen und den häufig Hunderten von Zeugnissen devianten Verhaltens aus dem Rechtsalltag der Orden. Zentrales Anliegen ist dabei die Aufdeckung von Anlässen, Auslösern und Spannungsfeldern, sowie der entsprechenden Reaktionen der Ordensinstanzen, der Strategien der Bewältigung und Prävention, der

Reflexe in Rechtsprechung, Rechtssetzung und Organisation. Nach signifikanten Traditionen, Unterschieden, Parallelen im Umgang beider Orden mit Devianz und Devianten wird dabei ebenso gefragt wie generell nach der Funktionalität abweichenden Verhaltens innerhalb monastischer Lebensformen.
Bd. 9, 2000, 384 S., 40,90 €, br., ISBN 3-8258-3443-3

Eliana Magnani Soares-Christen
Monastères et aristocratie en Provence – milieu X⁰ – début XII⁰ siècle
Au milieu du Xe siècle, la Provence sort d'une longue période de conflits politiques pendant laquelle les anciens monastères avaient presque entièrement disparu. La fondation de Montmajour et l'implantation des moines clunisiens en Haute Provence marquent le début d'une longue série de restaurations et de fondations de monastères bénédictins, dont Saint-Victor de Marseille et Lérins. Ce mouvement de renouveau est directement lié à l'action des familles aristocratiques qui s'investissent dans l'installation de communautés monastiques sur leurs domaines, alors même qu'elles érigent leurs seigneuries. Le rôle du monachisme bénédictin dans l'émergence et l'affirmation de l'ordre seigneurial est la question de départ de ce livre. Les monastères, dépositaires à la fois de l'identité sociale et de la mémoire patrimoniale des familles, sacralisent les nouveaux pouvoirs. Fondé sur la perméabilité des monastères vis-à-vis du monde laïque, le système de rapports établi entre les monastères et leurs bienfaiteurs est ébranlé par la réforme grégorienne. Au début du XIIe siècle, à l'issue de ce mouvement qui cherche à accentuer le clivage entre moines et laïcs et du succès de la première croisade, une autre forme de vie religieuse – celle qui, chez les ordres militaires, combine paradoxalement la vie consacrée du moine avec l'activité typique du chevalier – s'impose à l'horizon de l'aristocratie provençale.
Bd. 10, 1999, 632 S., 40,90 €, br., ISBN 3-8258-3663-0

Gert Melville; Jörg Oberste (Hg.)
Die Bettelorden im Aufbau
Beiträge zu Institutionalisierungsprozessen im mittelalterlichen Religiosentum
Die sich im frühen 13. Jahrhundert herausbildenden Bettelorden stehen, folgt man der traditionellen Ordensforschung, für eine radikale Umorien-

LIT Verlag Münster – Hamburg – Berlin – Wien – London
Grevener Str./Fresnostr. 2 48159 Münster
Tel.: 0251 – 23 50 91 – Fax: 0251 – 23 19 72
e-Mail: vertrieb@lit-verlag.de – http://www.lit-verlag.de

tierung in der mittelalterlichen vita religiosa. Die hier vorgelegten Ansätze einer vergleichenden Bestandsaufnahme zu den institutionellen Strukturen der frühen Mendikanten verdeutlichen, daß die Ordensbildung bei Franziskanern und Dominikanern stärker in einem Spannungsfeld zwischen innovativen und traditionellen Aspekten zu sehen ist. Die Studien, die sich vorrangig auf die erste Hälfte des 13. Jahrhunderts konzentrieren, entstanden im Rahmen des 1997 eingerichteten Forschungsprojektes "Institutionelle Strukturen religiöser Orden im Mittelalter" am Dresdner SFB 537, "Institutionalität und Geschichtlichkeit". Einem institutionenanalytischen Ansatz verpflichtet, wird die Genese und Etablierung der Bettelorden auf unterschiedlichen Ebenen untersucht. Ein Schwerpunkt des Sammelbandes liegt dabei auf der Frage nach der Herausbildung von Normensystemen und den Modi ihrer Geltungsdurchsetzung: Welchen spezifischen Leitvorstellungen fühlten sich die frühen Mendikanten verpflichtet? Welche Wege der Internalisierung und Verbreitung solcher Vorstellungen standen zur Verfügung? In welcher Weise verfestigten sich Ursprungsideale und soziale Funktionszuweisungen in den organisatorischen Strukturen der Orden? Wie wurden die neuen Gemeinschaften schließlich von ihrer Umgebung wahrgenommen? Die einzelnen Beiträge widmen sich charakteristischen Medien (z. B. Exempla) und Leitbegriffen (z. B. simplicitas) in der Frühphase der Bettelorden, ferner der Entwicklung ihrer organisatorischen Gestalt auf zentraler wie lokaler Ebene, den ideellen wie praktischen Grundlagen ihrer funktionalen Bestimmungen (z. B. Mission, Predigt) und nicht zuletzt den Bezugspunkten und Wurzeln im monastisch-kirchlichen Um- und Vorfeld. Untersuchungen zu den Cluniazensern, Zisterziensern und Hospitalorden, der Pariser Moraltheologie um 1200 und zum Pontifikat Papst Innozenz' III. stecken hier den vergleichenden Rahmen ab.
Bd. 11, 1999, 680 S., 45,90 €, br., ISBN 3-8258-4293-2

Florent Cygler
Das Generalkapitel im hohen Mittelalter
Cisterzienser, Prämonstratenser, Kartäuser und Cluniazenser
Die vorliegende Studie unternimmt eine historisch vergleichende Analyse der Organisationsformen und Funktionen des Generalkapitels im hohen

Mittelalter. Sie verfolgt das Ziel, dieses als (Sub-) Institution des okzidentalen Ordenswesens in seiner geschichtlichen Bedeutung sowie Diversität zu erfassen. Mit der Konzentration auf die Cisterzienser, Prämonstratenser, Kartäuser und Cluniazenser werden hierfür jene Orden in den Blick genommen, die in besonderer Weise die für Organisation und Identität zentrale Einrichtung des Generalkapitels geprägt und damit dem Religiosentum seit dem Hochmittelalter eine neue Verfaßtheit gegeben haben.
Bd. 12, 2002, 544 S., 40,90 €, br., ISBN 3-8258-4996-1

Gert Melville; Annette Kehnel (Hg.)
In proposito paupertatis
Studien zum Armutsverständnis bei den mittelalterlichen Bettelorden
Die freiwillige Armut bildet in ihren vielfältigen kulturhistorischen Verflechtungen ein nicht leicht überschaubares Feld: Armut als symbolische Darstellung von Weltverachtung und Gottesnähe; Armut als Ursprungsmythos religiösen Lebens; Armut als Komplexitätsreduktion, autorisiert durch den Rückbezug auf die vita apostolica bzw. die vita evangelica; Armut als Fundierung spiritueller wie organisatorischer Autorität; Armut als Provokation herrschender Diskurse und Gesellschaftsordnungen; Armut als stets abrufbares Reformprinzip; Armut als wirtschaftliches Problem, etc. Der vorliegende Band stellt diese Polyvalenz der optionalen Armut am historischen Beispiel mittelalterlicher Bettelorden erneut zur Diskussion und untersucht das propositum paupertatis zuerst und vor allem als ein konsumtives Legitimations- und Funktionsprinzip im Institutionalisierungsprozeß der Bettelorden. Sein Anliegen sähen die Herausgeber und Beitragenden in hohem Maße erfüllt, wenn die facettenreichen Überlegungen den ordensgeschichtlichen Diskursen über die Armut weitere Anstöße geben würden.
Bd. 13, 2001, 248 S., 25,90 €, br., ISBN 3-8258-5340-3

Jürgen Sarnowsky
Macht und Herrschaft im Johanniterorden des 15. Jahrhunderts
Verfassung und Verwaltung der Johanniter auf Rhodos (1421 – 1522)
Der geistliche Ritterorden der Johanniter war eine internationale Gemeinschaft, deren Mitglieder aus allen Teilen Europas kamen, aber gemeinsam im östlichen Mittelmeer kämpften und eine

LIT Verlag Münster – Hamburg – Berlin – Wien – London
Grevener Str./Fresnostr. 2 48159 Münster
Tel.: 0251 – 23 50 91 – Fax: 0251 – 23 19 72
e-Mail: vertrieb@lit-verlag.de – http://www.lit-verlag.de

Landesherrschaft in der Ägäis errichteten. Diese Untersuchung behandelt die Entwicklung von Regeln und Strukturen innerhalb des zentralen Konvents auf Rhodos sowie die Beziehungen zwischen dem Orden und seinen Untertanen, unter besonderer Berücksichtigung der tatsächlichen Verhältnisse des 15. Jahrhunderts und der aktuellen Diskussionen um "Macht" und "Herrschaft" in geistlichen Gemeinschaften. Während sich die älteren Verfassungsgeschichten des Ordens auf die normativen Quellen konzentrierten und zumeist von späteren Sammlungen ausgingen, baut diese Untersuchung auf einer Durchsicht aller relevanten Quellen im Johanniter-Archiv in der National Library of Malta in Valletta auf, ergänzt durch Materialien aus dem Archivio Segreto Vaticano, der Biblioteca Apostolica Vaticana, aus London, Paris und München.

Bd. 14, 2001, 760 S., 51,90 €, br., ISBN 3-8258-5481-7

Anne Müller

Bettelmönche in islamischer Fremde

Institutionelle Rahmenbedingungen franziskanischer und dominikanischer Mission in muslimischen Räumen des 13. Jahrhunderts

Mit ihrer erstaunlichen Mobilität erschlossen Bettelmönche völlig neue Aktionsräume auch jenseits der geographischen Peripherie der Christenheit. Das verschaffte ihnen Funktionszuweisungen, die das traditionelle Mönchtum nicht kannte. Auch die Mission unter den Heiden konnten die Bettelorden aufgrund ihrer universellen Verfügbarkeit für sich monopolisieren. Wie der Anspruch auf Heidenmission als ein zentraler Funktionsaspekt des Mendikantentums im institutionellen System des Franziskaner- und Dominikanerordens verankert und im Ordensalltag umgesetzt wurde, ist Gegenstand dieser Untersuchung. Am Beispiel des islamischen Wirkraums wird für das 13. Jahrhundert beleuchtet, welche Rolle die Predigt unter den Heiden im Gefüge ordensinterner Leitideen spielte, welche normativen und organisatorischen Strukturen zur Verstetigung dieses Anspruchs geschaffen wurden und wie sich der Geltungsrahmen der Heidenmission unter gewandelten geschichtlichen Bedingungen verschob.

Bd. 15, 2002, 360 S., 35,90 €, br., ISBN 3-8258-6159-7

Gert Melville, Markus Schürer (Hg.)

Das Eigene und das Ganze

Zum Individuellen im mittelalterlichen Religiosentum

„Das Individuelle" ist – ebenso wie seine Ableitungen „Individuum" und „Individualität" – ein zentraler Begriff abendländischen Denkens und somit Kristallisationspunkt einer Vielzahl theorie- und konzeptgeschichtlicher Diskurse. Zugleich ist mit ihm eine analytische Kategorie gegeben, deren erkenntnisstimulierende Wirkung innerhalb der aktuellen historischen, philosophischen, literaturwissenschaftlichen und soziologischen Forschungen ungebrochen ist, und die nicht zuletzt ganz spezifische wissenschaftliche Interessen im Bereich der Mediävistik markiert. Der vorliegende Sammelband will das Potential dieser Begriffe für die Untersuchung von Phänomenen aus dem weiten Bereich der mittelalterlichen *vita religiosa* nutzbar machen. Dabei verfolgen die einzelnen Beiträge eine Vielzahl verschiedener Perspektiven: Theoretisch orientierte Untersuchungen sind ebenso vertreten wie Fallstudien, die nach Formen der Selbsterkenntnis und -wahrnehmung des Menschen im Horizont göttlicher Transzendenz, nach Verfahren der Modellierung und Typisierung von Persönlichkeiten in hagiographischen und historiographischen Texten sowie nach den vielgestaltigen Varianten des Verhältnisses von Einzelnem und religiöser Gemeinschaft fragen.

Bd. 16, 2002, 728 S., 50,90 €, br., ISBN 3-8258-6163-5

Elke Goez

Pragmatische Schriftlichkeit und Archivpflege der Zisterzienser

Ordenszentralismus und regionale Vielfalt, namentlich in Franken und Altbayern (1098 – 1525)

Bd. 17, 2003, 408 S., 29,90 €, br., ISBN 3-8258-6491-x

LIT Verlag Münster – Hamburg – Berlin – Wien – London
Grevener Str./Fresnostr. 2 48159 Münster
Tel.: 0251 – 23 50 91 – Fax: 0251 – 23 19 72
e-Mail: vertrieb@lit-verlag.de – http://www.lit-verlag.de